W9-BGN-838

preparing for adolescence

how to survive the coming years of change

Dr. James Dobson

Gospel Light

Gospel Light

Gospel Light is a Christian publisher dedicated to serving the local church. We believe God's vision for Gospel Light is to provide church leaders with biblical, user-friendly materials that will help them evangelize, disciple and minister to children, youth and families.

It is our prayer that this Gospel Light resource will help you discover biblical truth for your own life and help you minister to youth. May God richly bless you.

For a free catalog of resources from Gospel Light, please contact your Christian supplier or contact us at 1-800-4-GOSPEL *or* www.gospellight.com.

EDITORIAL STAFF

Senior Managing Editor, Sheryl Haystead • **Writer,** William Stearns • **Contributing Editors,** Mary Davis, Linda Gray, Annette Parrish • **Art Director** Samantha A. Hsu • **Designer,** Rosanne Moreland

Founder, Dr. Henrietta Mears • **Publisher,** William T. Greig • **Senior Consulting Publisher,** Dr. Elmer L. Towns • **Senior Consulting Editor,** Wesley Haystead, M.S.Ed. • **Senior Editor, Biblical and Theological Issues,** Bayard Taylor, M.Div.

Library of Congress Cataloging-in-Publication Data
Dobson, James C., 1936-
   Preparing for adolescence group guide / James Dobson.
      p. cm.
   ISBN 0-8307-3829-0 (trade paper)
   1. Church work with teenagers. 2. Adolescence—Religious aspects—Christianity. 3. Adolescent psychology.
   4. Church group work. 5. Teenagers—Religious life. I. Title.
   BV4447.D6145 2005
   259'.23—dc22
                                                                                            2005027061

CONTENTS

WELCOME

WELCOME TO PREPARING FOR ADOLESCENCE

This 10-session course is designed to help students, ages 10-14, prepare for their teenage years.

During this course students will discover or review:

- how to handle feelings of inferiority
- how to develop self-confidence
- how to handle group pressure to conform
- how to say no to drugs and alcohol
- physical and sexual development
- the meaning of real love
- how to handle emotions
- how to make sound decisions
- understanding normal independence
- the basics of self-identity

PREPARING FOR ADOLESCENCE CAN BE USED FOR:

- Midweek program
- Youth retreats
- Youth camps
- Summer programs
- Saturday afternoons
- Sunday School
- Sunday evening program
- Youth groups
- Vacation Bible School

It is recommended that the class size be kept reasonably small and that the students and teacher have a previously developed trusting relationship.

Preparing for Adolescence is designed for students aged 10-14. Because the subject matter is highly personal, it is important that each student involved is developmentally ready. You may want to selectively offer this course to students, basing their attendance on maturity, not chronological age. (Many 10- and 11-year-old girls will be ready; most boys of that age will not.) Parents will appreciate being contacted to help in determining their child's readiness level. (NOTE: A reproducible parental consent form is included on p. 116.)

TEACHING HELPS

Course Overview

This course focuses on the wisdom of preparation for one of the most tumultuous periods in a person's life: adolescence. As students respond to Dr. Dobson's insights and their scriptural basis, they'll be preparing themselves to successfully cope with the challenges of teenage inferiority complexes, peer pressure, sexual and emotional development and the process of gaining independence.

Session 1: Caution! Bridge Out Ahead!
Biblical Basis: Psalm 22:1-18; Matthew 27:35-46

Focus: Feelings of inferiority are common in adolescence.

Session 2: Looks, Brains and Bucks
Biblical Basis: Psalm 139:13,14; Isaiah 53:2; Matthew 8:20; 27:39-42; Ephesians 2:10; Hebrews 6:18

Focus: Because God created each person with unique beauty and abilities, adolescents don't have to feel inferior for not measuring up to the world's standards of beauty, wealth and intelligence.

Session 3: The Canyon of Inferiority: Alternate Route Ahead
Biblical Basis: Exodus 4:10-14; Psalm 139:1-4,13-16; 2 Corinthians 12:7-10; James 1:2-4

Focus: With God's help, adolescents can deal with feelings of inferiority by changing what can be changed and accepting what can't be changed.

Session 4: Everybody's Doing It
Biblical Basis: Matthew 26:69-75; Acts 4:18-20; 7:58—8:1; 14:19; Romans 1:16; 12:1,2; 2 Corinthians 4:16-18

Focus: Renewed thinking and courage from God's Spirit can help adolescents resist pressure to conform.

Session 5: Something Crazy Is Happening to My Body!
Biblical Basis: Genesis 1:27,28; 2:20-25; Psalm 139:13-16; 1 Corinthians 6:18,19; Ephesians 5:31; 1 Thessalonians 4:3-8; Hebrews 13:4

Focus: An understanding of adolescent sexual development and the responsibilities it brings can help teenagers fulfill God's plan for their bodies.

Session 6: I Think I'm in Love!
Biblical Basis: 1 Corinthians 13:4-8a; Philippians 2:1-4; 1 John 4:7,8

Focus: Infatuation with a member of the opposite sex is normal during adolescence but is different from real love.

Session 7: Marriage: Drama in Real Life!
Biblical Basis: Genesis 2:18-24

Focus: Marriage isn't for kids; but adolescence is a good time to begin understanding the basics of a godly marriage.

Session 8: A Notion Called Emotion
Biblical Basis: Psalm 22:11; 100:1,2; Isaiah 21:4; Jeremiah 20:18; Romans 7:19; Hebrews 13:6

Focus: Although emotions are an important, God-given part of life, they must be balanced by sound judgment when making decisions.

Session 9: The Declaration of Independence
Biblical Basis: Ephesians 6:1-4

Focus: Adolescents can prepare for increasing freedom and responsibility by respecting, obeying and communicating with their parents.

Session 10: Who Am I?
Biblical Basis: Psalm 9:1; 139:14; Jeremiah 24:7; Matthew 28:19,20; 1 Corinthians 12:27; 2 Corinthians 3:18; Ephesians 1:4; 2:10; 1 Peter 2:9

Focus: God's Word provides wisdom and reassurance to adolescents who are struggling with questions about personal identity and purpose.

Things You Will Need for Teaching These Sessions

Technically, you don't have to have a copy of the *Preparing for Adolescence* text by James Dobson since the following Teacher Study sections summarize the book's content. But solid preparation will give confidence to your teaching, so having and studying the book as well as this manual is recommended.

Likewise, your students can get along without the book. But these life-changing lessons will be that much more effective if both youth and parent follow along in Dobson's book as you lead the group studies. The *Preparing for Adolescence Family Guide* provides an ideal structure to coordinate parents, youth and group study of these vital topics. Contact Gospel Light at www.gospellight.com to order these products.

Be sure to have in your classroom the following supplies and equipment for every session.

- Extra Bibles
- Pens or pencils
- Scratch paper
- A writing surface and something to write with—for example, a chalkboard with plenty of chalk, an overhead projector with transparencies and appropriate pens (Be sure to check whether these transparency pens

work!) or large sheets of butcher paper or newsprint (often available at no cost at your local newspaper production department) and felt markers.
- Individual session plans list any other materials you'll need for each learning activity—materials such as Student Worksheets, equipment for games, etc.

MAKING FLEXIBLE USE OF THE PREPARING FOR ADOLESCENCE COURSE

You can use this course for Vacation Bible School, summer camp or for a midweek program any time of year. Or you might plan a new structure especially for the *Preparing for Adolescence* program:

- Host a weekly or monthly *Preparing for Adolescence* get-together. During the evening or Saturday morning, preteens and their parents play together in recreation and crowd breaker activities. Then while the preteens work through the activities in this guidebook, their parents meet separately to review parenting skills and discuss how to reinforce the lessons at home. The *Preparing for Adolescence Family Guide* (Gospel Light) is available in Christian bookstores or from the publisher. It teaches parenting skills and includes reinforcing activities.
- Plan a retreat for the pre-adolescents of your church and community. Again, parents may be invited to attend their own concurrent sessions while at the retreat. Over a two-day retreat, plan to cover no more than four lessons—either the first four or last four, with the remaining lessons covered at home.
- Offer the course as a community service for preteens and their parents. Even families not involved in your church program may want help for their preteens, and many non-

Christian parents rely on Dr. Dobson's insights for raising healthy children. Hold the sessions in a neutral community building and invite unchurched parents to attend and help. Rather than using the course as an evangelistic forum, do your best to share the biblical principles of preparing for adolescence. Opportunities for actual evangelism will come later through the relationships you develop during the course.

- Feel free to adapt the program to your own time structure. Replace some activities with your own better ideas, choose a combination of Alternate activities that will fit your overall time limit, or use some of the following suggestions to customize your *Preparing for Adolescence* course.

Recreation

Physical activity is very important in any ministry to youth. Playing together expends energy that otherwise might be disruptive during a learning session. Recreation also quickly and naturally builds relationships among kids. By watching how adult supervisors act during games, youth catch the "tone" of adults' authority, of how much these adults care and how lovingly consistent they are in group discipline. Games also provide opportunities to learn and act out Christian principles of how to be fair, how to handle disagreements, how to have fun.

A few recreation tips to keep in mind:

1. Generally, have recreation first during a session. This allows latecomers to be incorporated in the activities without missing more important input: it loosens up newcomers and expends pent-up energy. But consider periodically scheduling your game time after the study period to avoid boring predictability.

2. Plan your games and gather necessary materials well in advance. Be at the game site before your students. This will give maximum game time and, from the outset, put you in comfortable control of the activity.

3. Use games that involve everybody—even the kids who never want to participate. The nonparticipating youth has his or her reasons for holding back (from not wanting to mess a perfect hairdo to sudden hatred for one of the opposing team members to having worn the wrong outfit or being too shy to admit a physical problem). Group games such as softball or volleyball can accommodate lots of players who simply want to stand around. Don't insist everyone be in the game itself, but do involve everyone by appointing kids as scorekeepers, timekeepers, equipment handlers, cheerleaders, team coaches or referees to watch boundaries.

4. Minimize competition. Organized sporting events cater to kids' desire to compete; group recreation is only for fun. Appoint teams yourself to avoid the popularity contest of letting kids choose teams. Since pre- and younger teenagers come in such diverse sizes, equalize the teams according to size as well as age and ability. If one side begins to lose miserably, stop the game and go on to another one. By regularly reorganizing teams from game to game or from one session to the next, no one group of youth begins to feel like the lowest caste of the youth world: the losers.

5. Generally, don't be a participant yourself. If you, parents or other adults are involved in a game, set limits to what the grownups can do. Kids need adults who will play *with* them, not grownup kids who compete with them.

6. Maintain your recreation equipment. Don't depend on kids to bring the materials or equipment; at one time or other they'll forget, they'll feel ashamed and you'll be left panicking to devise a game not requiring the equipment. Appoint a committee of youth to monitor balls, marker whistles, etc., and to put equipment away before study times.

7. Keep a well-stocked first aid kit nearby during recreation activities. Remember to take the kit with you when changing game sites. Have stenciled on the kit local emergency phone numbers for doctor, ambulance, fire, etc.

8. Surprisingly, rugged games can be played indoors. But remember: if anything near a preteen can get broken, it will. Clear out any valuable items from the entire room before launching into an active indoor game.

An additional resource from Gospel Light is OUT-RAGEOUS OBJECT LESSONS—will rivet your students' attention on the truth of God's Word. Contains over forty object lessons, each with tips and related Bible passages.

Crowdbreakers

Some leaders gain students' attention and build participation with quick activities called crowdbreakers. Crowdbreakers can provide a transition from recreation to serious study or be used as a replacement for recreation. A crowdbreaker often consists of a practical joke, a silly game played by a few people while others watch, or a fun, brief whole-group activity. Check your local Christian bookstore for crowdbreaker resource books. Keep in mind that some young adolescents revel in becoming the center of attention as the recipients of good-natured jokes while others would rather die than be even faintly embarrassed. The objective in crowdbreakers is to have fun, not make fun; so it's best to ask for volunteers for such events.

Skits are also good initial activities or transitions from game time to study time. The skits can be prepared by a few participants or adults, or they may be spontaneously assigned:

- Grab four others and in 45 seconds be prepared to act out a beauty-aid commercial while the rest of us guess the name of the product!
- You, you and you jump up and act out a family dinner where the kid asks for a new iPod!

Fellowship

Saying, "You *will* love each other and get along well" is hardly what will foster deep fellowship among your socially awkward preteens. Especially during this pre-adolescent age, kids can be cruelly cold to newcomers, ornery to the out-of-it regulars and even spiteful to their best friends. So it's going to take more than an announcement to help your youth establish friendly contact with newcomers and enjoy deepening fellowship in their *Preparing for Adolescence* study group. Try these approaches:

- Mix outsiders and insiders in recreation and indoor game activities. Being on a team together can help pre- and young teenagers get past externals such as appearance and recognize more important qualities in each other.
- Before and after your sessions, assign preparation and cleanup tasks to pairs or groups of students who normally don't hang around together.
- Sometimes seemingly snobbish or reserved kids simply need to learn social skills such as how to introduce someone. So teach some social skills: Make a point to introduce kids to each other. Then ask socially-adept regulars to introduce a newcomer to other kids.
- Talk privately with two or three regulars about how the group can better include a loner. These regulars may be bona fide insiders, but they do know how it feels to be left out and will themselves come up with several ideas. Avoid saddling one student with someone who is considered unpopular; youth often fear that if they befriend a loner, that kid will never let go. Having two or three regulars together befriend an outsider is much less threatening.
- Notice that many of the learning activities provide structures for kids to share in pairs or small groups. By regularly assigning students to specific partners or small groups, you can make sure these pairings aren't always just the same cliques of best friends.

Singing and Worship

Singing is usually a good way to bond a group of kids, to move the momentum of the session toward study time and to just have a good time together. Some tips to encourage hearty participation in a song time:

- Plan the number of songs (and verses of each) according to your time frame. Then adjust that number according to the disposition of the group at the session; sometimes they'll want to sing and sometimes they simply won't. You can't sing too few songs; one or two ripping songs will leave them wanting more. But you can sing too many; if they get bored with too many verses or too many songs, they'll probably stay bored throughout the lesson.

- Plan your songs according to their effect on the singers. A simple plan for each session's singing can move your kids from where they are (probably puffing with exertion from games and crowdbreakers) to where they need to be for an effective study session. Plan your song sequence with fast, less serious titles first and more thoughtful, worshipful songs last.

- Mix in one, or at most two, new songs in a session. Check with several kids to find out what songs they know and which are new to them. Feel free to include nonsacred favorites if they can contribute to the overall effectiveness of the song time and of the lesson.

- Have words printed on Power Point, song sheets or on overhead transparencies. Have just enough song sheets so kids must look on together in pairs. Make sure you pretest the projection of songs to check for visibility in all parts of the room.

- There are two essentials for those who lead music for youth groups—enthusiasm and volume! Even very self-conscious kids will often sing out if they have leaders who may drown them out. Conscript older teens or an adult, if necessary, or sing along to a music CD.

- If you're not a songleader, find an adult or older teenager who can direct this important activity with ease. This will conserve both your self-esteem and your kids' interest in *Preparing for Adolescence*!

- Choose your songs carefully, using them not just to fill time but to purposefully express significant ideas your students need to remember. Plan for a balance of familiar favorites and a few new songs.

Try one of these ideas to enliven your song times:

- Challenge small groups of students in-class to set the session's Key Verse to a familiar tune.

- Assign one or two musical students to, on their own time, create a song about trusting God. They can then teach this as a theme song to the rest of the group.

- Take time to stop and discuss the meanings and implications of phrases of a song; occasionally read a verse of the song rather than sing it.

But beware. Singing can also have a dampening effect on your get-together if the kids aren't used to singing together, if a majority of them simply don't like to sing, if the songs aren't interesting or known, and if they feel they *have* to sing. If your song time isn't working, drop singing and substitute something that has a broader appeal to your students. Do small group problem-solving, role-playing, brainstorming, conversational prayer, etc. Do what works best with your group to involve them in a meaningful time with God.

Prayer. Introduce your prayer time with a brief reminder that you as a group are about to address the God of the universe, the King of kings and Lord of lords. Suggest that students close their eyes as you describe an imaginary entrance into the very throne room of God. State that you as a spokesperson will present the group before the throne; then turn and actually concentrate on talking to God in behalf of your students.

Another way to avoid the perfunctory dullness of prayers that are only mini-sermons in disguise is to encourage group conversational prayer. Use everyday language yourself—while maintaining the sense that you're talking with Someone infinitely important.

Expect very few preteens to be comfortable when praying aloud in group situations. You can, however, involve them in prayer by joining hands and praying silently, by writing a one-sentence prayer which you or another adult reads, by voicing a group Amen after your prayer, or—as the Korean church does—praying aloud all at once so no one speaker feels intimidated.

Group Study

Learning the basics of *Preparing for Adolescence* and the biblical principles of growing up as God's teenagers is, of course, the focus of this course. So each session is packed with stimulating, tested group studies of biblical principles reflecting Dr. Dobson's insights.

It's critical that this learning segment of your course take into account the limited attention span of your learners. Preteens can handle about 10 minutes of sitting still. So your success in reaching your students with solid, biblical preparations for adolescence depends on how involved you keep them. The "hands-on" learning activities set out for each session may seem the long way around to a simple truth which you could simply tell your students. But keeping them active in learning assures first that they'll retain more and second that they'll be more cooperative in learning what God, Dr. Dobson and you have to teach. Don't allow passivity and boredom to rob your kids of valuable lessons on how to survive the teenage years intact!

Teaching

1. Review each lesson and work through the student activities yourself well in advance of the session.
2. Be the first to arrive in your classroom and the last to leave.
3. The learning environment is often a key factor in how well your students respond. Be sure to check room temperature. See that the room is clean and free from distracting items or noise. Simple factors such as proper ventilation and lighting can affect your kids' learning processes.
4. Enlist enough leaders to maintain about a 1 to 8 leader-to-student ratio. This will obviously ease your responsibility in maintaining effective learning throughout the session. Having adequate leaders will also ensure that, because of the personal nature of some of the materials you'll be covering, kids with special needs and questions won't be overlooked. If you don't yet have an adequate staff, consider recruiting several parents or older teenagers to work under your direction with small groups of students.
5. Display your students' handiwork on bulletin boards. Give them opportunities to share what they create. Be lavish in your praise as they try as much as they're capable to express their thoughts and feelings—whether it's by unrolling their butcher paper messages in an adult meeting or by videotaping a skit and showing it to younger groups. Let them know you care about their responses to what they're learning.
6. Enjoy a class that responds to your leadership. State at the onset a few necessary, specific rules for the course. For instance, state clearly that only one person may speak at a time, that instructions are given to be followed, that questions may be asked at any time by raising a hand, etc. Be sure that even as students watch or listen to a classmate, the visual focal point of control is an adult. Pre-adolescents left in the spotlight will quickly assume control and derail your session objectives. Establish yourself as the leader.
7. When—not if—you do experience a group discipline problem:

   • Lovingly, consistently face and handle problems before they escalate.
   • Immediately assign an adult to sit with the offender or in the middle of the offending group.

- If a student is consistently distracting others, physically remove or have another adult remove him or her from the group and one-on-one talk over the problem.
- Outside of class, make a contract with each disruptive student. Determine what he or she can do to enjoy the class without distracting others from preparing for the rigors of adolescence.
- Pray for the kids who haven't learned group discipline, and let them know you're consistently praying for them.

ABOUT INVOLVEMENT LEARNING

Adolescents find themselves in an interesting predicament: How do you enjoy life the way a child does when you're no longer a child? How do you handle a life with adult-sized problems when you're not yet an adult?

The awkward years of pre-adolescence are a period when many kids ask deep questions while giggling like six-year-olds. It's a precarious time, adults know, when kids are beginning to rationally form personal values, when they're struck with new, disturbing thoughts about self-identity, adult relationships, the reality of God.

And the hardest part is yet to come. Adolescence itself lies just ahead, with its intense emotions, sexual development and increasing peer pressures.

If we care about these vulnerable, challenging, lovable preteens, how can we help? Many adults think that the best we can do is tell kids what life is all about.

But try to remember what you felt about adult advice and lectures when you were 12. Yes, that was ages ago; but doubtless you remember sessions in which well-meaning adults tried to stuff wisdom in your ear through long talks and lectures. And you know it went in one ear only to go out the other.

It's not enough to tell kids about God's plans for their teenage years. Many successful children's and youth workers have found that much more is retained when kids are guided to discover truths for themselves in active involvement learning.

Involvement Learning

The teaching methods and materials in this book emphasize involvement learning. These methods will keep your students busy; they'll be active learners rather than passive listeners.

Each session in this Group Guide includes three activities:

- **Approach to the Word**—involves students in activities that capture and direct their interest toward the session theme.
- **Bible Exploration**—suggests a variety of methods to learn what the Bible says about the session topic.
- **Conclusion**—involves each student in an activity that applies biblical truths to the real-world challenges of surviving adolescence.

To provide flexibility, each session includes alternate Approach, Exploration and Conclusion activities. That way, you can choose activities that best fit your time schedule, the maturity level of your group or simply your preferences.

The overall purpose of your group study is probably best summarized by Dr. Dobson's own parting message to his pre-adolescent readers in *Preparing for Adolescence*: "The . . . most important advice I can give you is to remain friends with Jesus Christ during the years ahead. When you face the important issues of life, He will guide your footsteps."

CHECK HOW YOU'RE DOING

Immediately following each session:

1. Review the session aims. Did you help your kids accomplish the aims? How do you know those goals were reached? If not, why not? What could have been changed? To what degree are you *sure* students understood the session's main points?
2. Evaluate your use of time. Were you able to work through what you'd planned, or did time get away from you? Did you give students enough time to complete the learning

activities? How can you better time the next session?

3. Were the learning activities, questions and concepts the right level for your group? Did some of their questions or comments suggest that they didn't feel the lesson pertained to them? How can you adjust to the maturity level and needs of the group for the next session?

4. Think back on students' participation. Who talked? Who didn't and why? Did you ask questions to draw out the nontalkers? What questions received immediate, real answers? How can you encourage more participation?

5. How well are you getting to know your students as individuals? What are their interests, needs and problems? What is their level of spiritual growth? What problems are they having? You can obviously target your lesson points toward meeting your kids' needs only if you get to know those actual needs. Plan times to talk with your students one-on-one. Jot in a journal what you know about each student, what you need to know and how you plan to follow up on helping to address each student's needs.

6. How did the session Scripture affect you in your own study? Were you involved in the theme of the session and enthusiastic about the activities you were directing? If not, how can you improve? Your students will only be as interested in the lesson as you are!

7. Pray specifically for your students' responses to the session. And pray for the effectiveness of the next session. Share your feelings of joy, panic, irritation and encouragement with the Lord; He's not only interested in these young lives, He's also vitally concerned with you.

How to Use This Course

No one knows your students as well as you do. So you're the final authority on exactly how to help them prepare for adolescence by following sound biblical and psychological principles.

Feel free to customize this material according to the needs of your students. The course material is presented in the three sections of this manual: The **Teacher's Manual Section** gives you directions for the ten study sessions. The **Student Worksheet Section** provides reproducible worksheets. The **Design-It-Yourself Section** contains other materials you can use in and outside class times to promote activities, decorate the room, add to the worksheets, etc. Let's take a closer look at each of these sections.

Teacher's Manual Section

Each session plan contains the **Key Verse**, **Biblical Basis**, **Focus**, **Aims**, **Teacher's Study and Session Teaching Plan**. The **Teacher's Study** provides you with a brief summary of the appropriate section of *Preparing for Adolescence*. It also gives you the scriptural background information you need to present the lesson.

Each *Session Plan* gives two options for the:

- **Approach**—to catch students' interest;

- **Exploration**—to examine the *Preparing for Adolescence* text as well as Scripture and its meaning for your students' lives; and the

- **Conclusion**—which guides students in making personal application of the insights from the session.

Student Worksheets

This section allows you to customize the course. These reproducible pages can be used as is or as you'd like them to be! Depending on which alternate learning activities you choose for your class, you can:

- Use them as is. The Student Worksheets are perforated, so you can simply tear them out of the manual and photocopy the necessary number of worksheets for your expected attendance. Be sure to make several extra copies for newcomers and visitors.

- Customize them. Photocopy and then cut up the worksheets; cut out portions you won't be using. Add more Bible passages, questions, comments, announcements or quotations. The material is copyrighted, but permission is given for you to use and photocopy the worksheets as you wish. (This legal permission to copy does not apply to the Teacher Manual Section.) Plan ahead and be creative with these worksheets. Use the materials selectively, zeroing in on the maturity level and needs of your students.

Design-It-Yourself Section!

In this section you'll find cartoons, illustrations and various messages that have absolutely nothing to do with the lessons in the Teacher's Manual Section. These pages are for fun—for creating professional-looking mailers, leaflets, posters, bulletins, newsletter announcements and decorations for Student Worksheets. Use some of the design elements to create customized stationery or postcards for your group. Have students who arrive especially early or who want extra responsibility help create some of these resources. Simply cut, paste or tape and add your own lavish artwork. Then photocopy or have a quick-print shop produce your masterpieces!

Keep your focus on teaching students, not teaching lesson materials. The editors of this guide along with Dr. Dobson join with you in our concern for kids. We're not so much excited about lesson plans being followed as we are about your disciplining younger adolescents toward a biblically-based teenage lifestyle.

SNACKS

Each day vary the refreshments you provide. The following nutritional and not-so-nutritional refreshment suggestions go beyond the usual punch and cookies. The suggestions marked with a star ☆ can be prepared by the students during snack time. NOTE: If you have students who have food allergies, make sure to bring an alternate snack for them.

☆ 1. *Banapple Salad*—Combine sliced bananas and pineapple chunks in a bowl. Spoon into paper cups. Top with dressing made by shaking together in a jar: $\frac{1}{2}$ cup plain yogurt, 2 tablespoons peanut butter and 2 tablespoons honey.

2. *Crispie Treats*—Butter a 9 x 12-inch (22.5 x 30-cm) baking pan and set aside. Place 4 cups miniature marshmallows, $\frac{1}{3}$ cup butter or margarine and $\frac{3}{4}$ cup peanut butter in a saucepan over low heat. Stir until all are melted together. Pour in 5 cups crispy rice cereal and stir gently to combine all ingredients. Pour mixture into pan and press down with spoon. Let cool and cut into squares.

☆ 3. *Berry Crunchy Yogurt*—Spoon vanilla yogurt, sliced strawberries or blueberries and Grape-Nuts into paper cups. Mix with a spoon and enjoy!

☆ 4. *Cheesy Cucumber Sandwiches*—Wash cucumbers, cut off ends and slice. Put cottage cheese between two slices to make small sandwiches.

5. *Sprouts in a Blanket*—Place a slice of luncheon meat and a slice of cheese on a lettuce leaf. Top with alfalfa sprouts. Sprinkle with Italian salad dressing. Roll up and secure with a toothpick.

☆ 6. *Applenutty Treats*—Mix peanut butter with apple sauce and serve on cinnamon graham crackers.

☆ 7. *Sparkling Apple Juice*—Stir together in a large pitcher a 12-oz. can apple juice concentrate, 32-oz. bottle club soda and 24 oz. water. Makes 17 4-oz. servings.

8. *Charoses*—Mix $\frac{1}{4}$ cup finely chopped nuts, 1 grated apple, $\frac{1}{4}$ cup grape juice and 1 teaspoon cinnamon. Serve with unleavened bread (matzo) or rice crackers.

9. *Yogurt Popsicles*—Blend together 1 cup plain yogurt, 1 sliced banana, 1 teaspoon vanilla, 1 cup fruit juice. Pour into small paper cups and freeze. When mixture is half frozen, place a Popsicle stick in each cup. To serve, turn cup upside down and run hot water over it until popsicle slips out. Makes 4 to 5 small popsicles.

10. *Tortilla Triangles*—Cut flour tortillas into six triangular pieces. Spread with mustard and sprinkle with grated cheese. Starting at large end, roll the triangle up and secure with a toothpick. Bake at 350°F for five minutes. Cool slightly and serve.

☆ 11. *Easy S'mores*—For each s'more, spread one graham cracker square with a layer of canned chocolate frosting. Spread a second graham cracker with marshmallow cream. Put together sandwich-style and enjoy.

☆ 12. *Orange Delight*—For each serving, blend together in a blender: ¼ cup orange juice concentrate, ½ cup plain yogurt and ½ cup milk. (A banana maybe substituted for yogurt.) Serve in paper cups.

CRAFT PROJECTS FOR YOUTH GROUPS

"Oh sure! Craft projects for my youth group. They'd sooner swim with alligators! *I'd* sooner swim with alligators!"

WAIT! Don't turn the page yet! We have actually had reports from some youth workers that craft projects were a BIG HIT with their young people. (These youth leaders aren't quite ready to release their names for publication. Social stigma and all that . . . you understand.)

Anyway, these leaders found the following to be true:

1. Young people will groan and roll their eyes heavenward when told, "We're going to make a craft now."

2. To keep the respect of your youth group, never say the word craft. That word is the ultimate no-no.

3. It is possible for your youth group to "do crafts" and enjoy it—without the word "craft" ever being mentioned. Simply say something like this: "I'm ready for a little change of pace. Let's move into the rec room [or over to the art tables, or wherever] and try our hands at a little creative mischief."

This creative break need not be a break from the focus of the session. It's a great time for you, the youth worker, to model concepts that have just been studied. It's also an excellent time to have casual conversation about the application of the concepts.

4. The end result (finished product) isn't nearly as important as the process of being creative and having a fun time with each other.

During this time of informal interaction, the youths develop new friendships and strengthen existing friendships. It's also within this informal context that you can better look at the personalities of your young people. Your ministry effectiveness will be enhanced as you become more aware of the individual spiritual and emotional needs of those in your youth group. So don't be appalled at the thought of embarking upon "craft projects" with those wild and woolly youth the Lord has temporarily put in your hands. Why don't you try some of this creative diversion and see for yourself. The possibilities for projects are limitless.

GAMES

Gooey Name Game

Materials: For each team: a pump-style tube of toothpaste, a large sheet of dark-colored paper, tape and a large drop cloth.

Procedure: Tape each sheet of colored paper on a wall at one end of the room. Place drop cloths on the floor beneath each sheet of paper. Divide class into teams. Have each team line up facing a sheet of paper on the opposite side of the room. Give the first person on each team a pump-style toothpaste tube. When teacher gives signal, the first person on each team runs to the paper and writes with toothpaste his or her first name. The player then runs back to team and passes the toothpaste to the next player. The first team to complete its list of names is the winner.

Sock Pass

Materials: One sock for each team.

Procedure: Two or more teams line up single file. A sock is given to the first person on each team. When the leader gives a signal, teams compete to pass the sock from one member to the next down the line. Each player may allow only one hand to touch the sock and sock must be pulled tightly over each player's hand before it is a legal pass (see sketch).

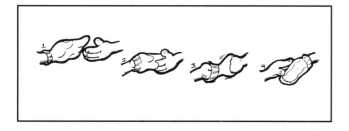

Cotton Ball Contest

Materials: Masking tape and several dozen cotton balls.

Procedure: Use masking tape to mark a line on the floor. Place cotton balls on the line. Divide class into two teams. Teams line up on each side of line, kneeling with hands behind backs. For a designated period of time, teams attempt to blow cotton balls to the opposite side of the line. When teacher signals that the game is over, the team with the fewest cotton balls on its side of the line wins.

Three-Team Tug-of-War

Materials: Two or three ropes and three scraps of cloth.

Procedure: Tie two or three ropes together to form a three-handled rope (see sketch). Make sure the knot is tied securely and will not pull apart during the game. Divide class into three teams. Each team assembles, holding on to one of the three ropes, as in a standard tug-of-war game. Mark three spots on the ground with scraps of cloth (see sketch). Teams compete to pull the knot in the rope over their spot. The team that does so wins.

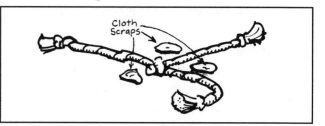

Skateboard Train Race

Materials: Skateboards and chairs or pylons.

Procedure: Mark off a race track with chairs or pylons. Divide class into teams of four. Three team members from each team sit on skateboards and hold onto each other to form "trains" (see sketch). The fourth team member from each team pushes the "train" as teams race against each other on the track. When players fall off, they must quickly reassemble and continue on. The "train" to cross the finish line first is the winner.

Skateboard Buddy Race

Materials: Skateboards.

Procedure: Each student chooses a "buddy" to race with. One buddy holds on to skateboard with his or her hands while "buddy" holds his or her feet and pushes (see sketch). Buddies race to cross a finish line.

Pull Party

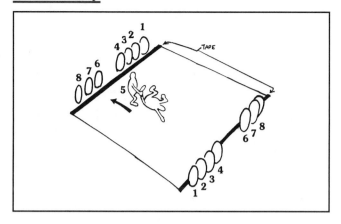

Materials: Masking tape.

Procedure: Place lines of masking tape on opposite sides of playing area. Divide class into two teams. Beside masking tape, each team lines up according to height (see sketch). Assign a number to the players on each team. Teacher begins game by calling out a number at random, such as "five." The two players assigned the number "five" run to the center of the playing area. These players compete, trying to pull the opponent over his or her line. The first player to succeed wins that round for his or her team. If two players are having a difficult time making progress, you may want to call in other players to assist them. This is a rugged game, so caution players to avoid unnecessary roughness.

preparing for
adolescence
group guide

Unit 1/Sessions 1-5

CAUTION! BRIDGE OUT AHEAD!

KEY VERSE

He has not despised or disdained the suffering of the afflicted one; he has not hidden his face from him but has listened to his cry for help. Psalm 22:24

BIBLICAL BASIS

Psalm 22:1-18; Matthew 27:35-46

PREPARING FOR ADOLESCENCE TEXT

First section of chapter 1

FOCUS OF THE SESSION

Feelings of inferiority are common in adolescence.

AIMS OF THIS SESSION

During this session each learner will:

- EXAMINE biblical examples of the ridicule experienced by King David and Jesus Christ;
- IDENTIFY his or her own negative and positive characteristics;
- PRAY for God's help in remembering and strengthening the positive characteristics.

TEACHER'S STUDY

To Be Young Again?

James Dobson begins his book *Preparing for Adolescence* with: "How would you like to be thirteen years old again?" He writes that he can "almost hear adult readers answering that question in one booming voice: 'No thanks!' Everyone in our culture wants to remain young, but not that young! . . . We have not forgotten the self-doubt and feelings of inferiority which seemed unbearable at times. And of course, we recall the emotional vulnerability to practically everything throughout adolescence—vulnerability to failure, to ridicule, to embarrassment."

Preparing for **Preparing for Adolescence**

Some of those feelings may not be easy for you to recall, just as they're not easy for your students to admit!

This session will give your students a glimpse of ways intimidating topics such as inferiority feelings can be simply and clearly brought out into the open. Most preteens and older youth alike find it difficult to ask adults how to handle feeling bad about themselves. Talking itself is often tough for young teenagers. They often can't find the right words to express deep feelings and questions such as those discussed in this session.

It is important to be aware of what your students are feeling—even if they seem distant, disinterested or fairly unresponsive. How will you know what they're feeling? By remembering what you felt. The externals of styles and activities change with every generation, but the internal feelings and struggles of growing up are the same for your students as they were back in the ancient history of your teenage years! Here are some suggestions to prepare for this session and the entire course:

- Determine what year you were 12 or 13.
- Spend a few hours in your public library browsing through that year's almanac, yearbook, magazines or stone tablets.
- Rummage through some of your old scrapbooks, school yearbooks, photo albums and diaries. Take note of your old school papers—especially any drawings or doodles of yourself. During this session your students will be designing a car to represent themselves, so keep in mind that self-portraits and other artwork often provide startling insights into how your students feel about themselves.
- Talk with old friends and family members to get your bearings on what happened during those years and to recall what you were like.

Slowly, or perhaps with bursts of memory, you'll begin reliving the crazy, painful, ecstatic woes and joys of becoming a teenager who's becoming an adult. Dr. Dobson points out: "Preteens can profit from what we have learned because we've been where they're going."

For this session, focus on incidents when you were criticized or ridiculed. Think through the details of the memories; the feelings will surprisingly surface. Those are the feelings your students will be focusing on during the session.

Be aware that your preteens won't easily admit or express their self doubts. Also, don't expect overnight changes in your students and exclamations of "Ah, yes. Now I'm confident of my self-worth even when others make fun of me!" Building self-confidence is a deep process that takes time, not quick behavioral change.

The Dark Canyon

Dr. Dobson suggests the way to begin preparing for adolescence is with a mental game. He tells the preteens to imagine driving down the highway toward Adultsville after passing through a little town by the name of Liberty. Suddenly a flagman stops the teenager with the warning that a bridge has collapsed ahead, leaving a huge drop-off into a dark canyon. With caution, dropping off into that canyon can be avoided—teenagers don't have to fall into the "Canyon of Inferiority."

Inferiority is a feeling of hopelessness, a feeling that nobody likes you, that you're not as good as other people, that you're a loser, that you're ugly, unintelligent or don't have much ability. It's a depressing feeling of worthlessness.

Everyone at some time feels threatened by inferiority. But some preteens, teenagers and even adults feel inferior and unworthy nearly all the time. Day after day they wish that they were someone else or that they could just disappear. Perhaps some of your students are feeling that way this week.

Those feelings of inferiority are amplified by the real or imagined negative comments, snide remarks, taunts and outright cruelty that seem to be inevitable factors of growing up.

The Inferior King

Many of your preteens like to identify with the familiar stories of young David who was strong enough to kill a lion, ruddy and healthy-looking, musically talented and brave enough to take on the giant Philistine, Goliath. Yet they might be surprised to find that this young man, who seemed to have everything going for him, occasionally felt severely depressed as his enemies taunted and ridiculed him. David was called *a man after God's own heart* (see 1 Samuel 13:14). He wasn't at all an inferior person; yet he acutely felt the jabs of those scorning him.

King David began Psalm 22 with, *My God, my God, why have you forsaken me? Why are you so far from saving me, so far from the words of my groaning?* Be sure to read through the entire psalm to catch the surges of David's feelings of inferiority mixed with his cries of dependence on the Lord.

The Superior King

Especially remarkable about David's lament is the repetition of portions of the psalm by another biblical character who was in no way inferior: Jesus Christ Himself! Some Bible commentators think that Jesus may have quoted the entire 22nd Psalm as He hung on the cross. Notice the prophetic details paralleled in the Psalm and in Matthew 27:35-46. *In Christ all fullness of the Deity lives in bodily form* (Colossians 2:9), so it seems unbelievable that people would make fun of Him as if He were inferior!

That an admirable character like King David and even the perfect God-man Jesus Christ were ridiculed should suggest to your students that they too will be painfully criticized at times during their teenage years.

Invariably, someone will hit them with a message that they don't match up to expectations.

More to Come

Dealing directly with such deep personal feelings is perhaps new to your students. So be prepared for reactions that may seem like indifference. But they are listening; they'll realize that self-doubt is common, that adults such as a King David or even a teacher can admit to such feelings and that feelings of inferiority can be talked over with a Savior who knows what it feels like to be put down (see Hebrews 4:15).

Whereas this session details the characteristics and the pitfalls of the Canyon of Inferiority, we won't leave your students hanging there on the edge of a cliff. Sessions two and three will equip them to avoid the Canyon of Inferiority—or in the case of some, to start climbing up out of it!

SESSION 1
TEACHING PLAN

APPROACH

Choose one Approach to help students consider preparing for the perils of a trip through the jungles of junior high and beyond.

APPROACH *(12-15 minutes)*

Materials needed: Copy for each student of the "Off to Bunga-bungaland" Student Worksheet 1, pencils.

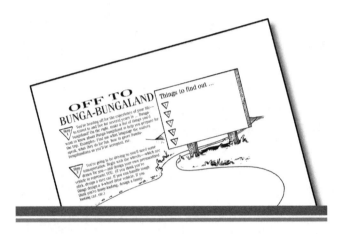

Distribute pencils and worksheets. Ask students to imagine that they will soon be traveling to a land called Bunga-bungaland. Instruct students to complete Step 1 on the worksheet in order to prepare for the trip. Allow volunteers to share their answers. Next, have each student complete Step 2—designing a vehicle that represents him or her.

For Step 3 say, **Now imagine that on your trip you come upon a bunch of bullies who say insulting things about you or your car. Inside the conversation balloons write what the bullies might say.** Lead into the Exploration by saying, **All of you are traveling into territory that's a lot more wonderful and, at the same time, frightening than Bunga-bungaland. You'll be traveling through years of being a teenager, and it only makes sense to prepare for your trip! That's exactly what we'll be talking about today.**

ALTERNATE APPROACH *(8-10 minutes)*

Materials needed: Chalkboard, chalk, paper, pencils.

Announce an actual outing which you and your students will take within the next few weeks (e.g., picnic, in-line skating, hiking, etc.). List these categories of preparations on the chalkboard: location, transportation, food, activities, equipment needed, reservations, publicity, costs. Divide class into two or more small groups. Give each group paper and a pencil and have them jot down their ideas (plan) for each category.

After several minutes, call the teams back to order even if they haven't finished brainstorming their plans. Say, **Most of you didn't have time to plan every detail of our trip, and we'll have to make better preparations for the trip to go smoothly. It's the same way for the trip each of you will be taking through your teenage years—a smooth trip of growing up takes planning and preparation.**

EXPLORATION

Use one of the following Explorations to help your students realize the threat that feelings of inferiority bring to adolescents.

EXPLORATION *(40-50 minutes)*

Materials needed: Bibles, copy for each student of the "Even David and Jesus?" Student Worksheet 2, pencils, tape recorder, blank cassette tape.

Teacher Preparation: Arrange to have an older teenager or one of your students act the part of the Troubled Teen. The Troubled Teen's monologue can be a paraphrase of the one found in *Step 1*. Have a male friend, whose voice your students won't recognize, tape-record the paraphrasing of Psalm 22, found in *Step 3*. The tone of the reading should be hurt, almost angry.

Step 1: Dramatization. Immediately after the Approach activity, wander across the front of the room and stop beside the Troubled Teen. Ask the youth what's bothering him or her and ad lib until the teenager blurts out something like: "Look, I've been going to school in this district for eight years, but I've never managed to make a single friend! Not one. I walk to school by myself and I walk home alone. I don't go to any school activities because I am embarrassed to sit there all alone. I eat lunch all by myself in a corner of the cafeteria. I don't get along with my dad, and my mom doesn't understand me. I have nobody! My phone never rings. Nobody cares anything about me. It seems like all people do is make fun of me. Sometimes I think I just can't stand it anymore."

After this dramatization, address the group, **Have you ever felt that way? That nobody cares? If you haven't yet, you probably will. Sometime during your teenage years someone might make fun of you, and you'll feel bad about yourself. It's as if you're driving along on the road to becoming an adult, then you come to a great big canyon. The bridge is out and over you go—down into a black hole where you feel really bad about yourself, where you're afraid that people will make fun of you. The canyon has been called The Canyon of Inferiority, and if you're not prepared for it, you may find yourself IN it! That's why we're all here together—to plan for the important years ahead.**

Step 2: Discussion. Say, **One thing that can easily put a person into the Canyon of Inferiority is put-downs. What are some ways you have seen others put down?** (Allow students to answer.)

Step 3: Pop Quiz. Say, **Listen to find out what famous person felt alone and put-down.** Play the recording of the paraphrase of portions of Psalm 22:

Oh, dear God, where are you when I need you? It seems like I'll never feel better again. You never answer my prayers. I've heard all the stories about how you answered the prayers of everybody in the Bible. I guess they weren't disappointed like I am. I don't even feel human sometimes. Everybody who looks at me makes fun of me. They sneer and shake their heads. It feels as if there's nobody to help me. My heart feels as if it's melting away like wax. I might as well be dead. (See Psalm 22:1,2,4-7,11,14,15.)

Take a quick survey to see who knows the identity of the speaker—King David.

Step 4: Student Worksheet 2. Direct students to find partners. Give each pair a Bible, a pencil and a copy of Student Worksheet 2.

Say, **King David isn't the only one in the Bible who felt alone and put-down. Work together to find out about the experiences and feelings Jesus shared with King David.**

Allow 10-12 minutes for study, then call for findings. Supplement students' comments with insights from this session's Teacher's Study. Emphasize that neither King David nor certainly the Lord Jesus Christ was inferior, yet others made fun of each of them.

ALTERNATE EXPLORATION
(50-60 minutes)

Materials needed: Bibles, a copy of "Even David and Jesus?" Student Worksheet 2 for each student, butcher or shelf paper, tape, pencils and felt markers.

Teacher Preparation: Tape a huge sheet of paper on a wall and letter the heading, "Ancient Warnings—Put-downs from 4,000 and 2,000 years ago!" Invite two or three older teenagers and adults to share with the group the feelings and experiences they encountered at the Canyon of Inferiority.

Step 1: Interviews. Interview your guests about the specific incidents and feelings they experienced as young teenagers in the Canyon of Inferiority. You may want to use interview questions such as: **What was one thing you were embarrassed about as a teenag-**

er? Tell us about a time others put you down. What might have helped you feel better about yourself?

Step 2: Student Worksheet 2. Pass out Bibles, pencils and Student Worksheets. Say, **Everyone experiences how it feels to be put down, even the people we study about in the Bible—and even Jesus! Instruct students to complete worksheet.**

Step 3: As students complete worksheet, ask volunteers to write on "Ancient Warning" sign any put-downs they find in the Bible passages studied in *Step 2.*

CONCLUSION

Choose a conclusion activity to help students emphasize their good qualities and increase their awareness of God's presence.

CONCLUSION *(10-12 minutes)*

Materials needed: Pencils and paper.

Distribute a sheet of paper and a pencil to each student. Instruct students to fold paper in half. On one side they list things they don't like about themselves. On the other side, they list what they do like about themselves. Assure students that they will not be required to show the list to anyone.

When students have completed their lists say, **You've each experienced being put down and you have characteristics you wish were different about yourself. But God gave each of you good characteristics that you can be thankful for. The next time you start feeling inferior, get out your list and read over the things you like about yourself. Ask a friend, teacher or family member to add to the list things they like about you.**

Students make check marks by two of the things they like best about themselves, then pray silently for help in remembering those good qualities when feelings of inferiority start to creep in.

Conclude with a prayer that assures your students that you know the pain and loneliness that accompany feelings of inferiority—when you're not actually inferior at all! Thank God for each person's good qualities.

ALTERNATE CONCLUSION *(8-10 minutes)*

Materials needed: Bibles, pencils, small index cards.

Pass out index cards and pencils to students. Direct students to turn in their Bibles to Psalm 22 and copy verse 24. Suggest each student memorize the verse and place the index card in a schoolbook or display it in his or her room. It can be a reminder that God is always there to help, even when feelings of inferiority creep in.

Each student turns index card over and writes two characteristics he or she likes about him or herself. Then each student prays silently that God will help him or her remember those good qualities when feelings of inferiority start to creep in. Conclude prayer by emphasizing that part of the preparation for growing up is facing times when people try to make us feel inferior. At those times, even if it seems He doesn't listen to us, God hears our cries.

EXTRA FEATURES

Add additional activities to your session to increase the impact of the lesson and—especially at this first session—to promote a feeling of fellowship.

Games—see page 15.
Snacks—see page 14.
Crafts—see page 15.

LOOKS, BRAINS AND BUCKS

KEY VERSE

The Lord does not look at the things man looks at. Man looks at the outward appearance, but the Lord looks at the heart. 1 Samuel 16:7

BIBLICAL BASIS

Psalm 139:13,14; Isaiah 53:2; Matthew 8:20; 27:39-42; Ephesians 2:10; Hebrews 6:18

PREPARING FOR ADOLESCENCE TEXT

Middle section of chapter 1

FOCUS OF THE SESSION

Because God created each person with unique beauty and abilities, adolescents don't have to feel inferior for not measuring up to the world's standards of beauty, wealth and intelligence.

AIMS OF THIS SESSION

During this session each learner will:

- COMPARE society's impossible standards for what's valuable in people with God's view of a person's value;
- TELL what the Bible says about the worth of people He has created;
- ASK God for help in believing what the Bible says about his or her worth.

TEACHER'S STUDY

The following commentary is for your own background study and review. Don't try to teach everything here to your students. You won't have time! The Session Plan specifies student learning activities that use some of this material.

Cultural Values vs. God's Values

This session's topic is one to which both teenagers and adults can easily relate. Regardless of your age group, you know and often feel society's pressures.

The media is a powerful influence, shaping our view of what makes a person valuable.

Attractive looks, money and possessions, intelligence and talent are the measuring sticks teenagers use to rate their peers. These same categories are often used by your own age group as measuring sticks to determine the value and success of people. Simply compare the ads in a teenage magazine with those in adults' magazines—they advertise different versions of the same message: To be loved and respected you need "looks, bucks and brains." It's typical to measure ourselves against this standard and become discouraged or depressed when we realize we don't measure up. We translate that to mean we are failures or of lesser value.

However, this standard we are so adept at using is not based on truth or a realistic view of life. The truth is that each human being is of infinite value and has virtually unlimited potential. In addition, each person has both strengths and weaknesses. Even the "beautiful people" in magazine and TV ads have weaknesses that they must deal with in life. The truth is that *no one* has it all.

Mother Nature's Damage

Dr. Dobson in *Preparing for Adolescence* suggests that teenagers in our culture feel they must have looks, possessions and abilities in order to feel good about themselves. "The first of these, and by far the most important," he says, "is physical attractiveness. Did you know that 80 percent of the teenagers in our society don't like the way they look?"

Remember studying yourself in the mirror hour after hour, practicing expressions, holding up hand-mirrors to see what you looked like from the side?

The teenage years are a time of determining identity. Visualizing how one looks to others is an important part of shaping that sense of "This is who I am." But preoccupation with appearance often gets out of hand during adolescence: "They feel ugly and unattractive," notes Dobson, "and they think about that problem most of the time. They also believe the opposite sex doesn't like them. The girls feel too tall and the boys feel too short, or they feel too fat or too thin or they're worried about the pimples on their faces or about the freckles on their noses or the color of their hair . . . No matter how minor the problem is, it can create great anxieties and depression."

It's important for younger adolescents to know that it's normal to feel dissatisfied with the shape and attractiveness of their bodies at some time in their teenage years.

Our Bodies in Scripture

Just because the world overemphasizes physical attractiveness doesn't mean, of course, that there is anything wrong with looking good! In fact, the story from which our key verse is taken ends with Samuel anointing young David as the future king—David who was *ruddy, with a fine appearance and handsome features* (1 Samuel 16:12). Other biblical characters are noted for their beauty (see Genesis 12:10-14; 24:15,16, for examples). So when considering the topic with adolescents, don't pressure them to swing from the world's overemphasis on physical attractiveness to an equally unbiblical overemphasis on the virtues of appearing as homely and unattractive as possible!

Still, the Bible teaches that what we look like is far less important than who we are. The fact that virtually nothing is recorded in the Bible about the physical appearance of Jesus Christ should tell us something about the relative value of our facial features and body shapes. The historian Josephus came closest to giving a physical description of the Lord when he reported that Jesus was tall, about a head taller than the average Judean. The physical description we do have in Scripture is found in a prophetic passage that perhaps describes Jesus as He hung on the cross or as He appeared throughout His earthly life—One who *had no beauty or majesty to attract us to him, nothing in his appearance that we should desire him* (Isaiah 53:2).

In our externally oriented society, junior highers, high schoolers, collegians and adults all regularly need to be reminded:

- God designed our bodies (Psalm 139:13,14);
- by His Spirit God can indwell our bodies (1 Corinthians 6:19,20); and
- someday we'll have new, perfect bodies (1 Corinthians 15:42-44,49-52).

Encourage students to discover things about their appearance that they can appreciate. Also preteens may not be aware that there are ways they might improve their appearance (i.e., keeping clean, eating right, exercising and dressing neatly). There is nothing wrong with making the most of what God has given each individual.

Intelligence and Ability

When it comes to intelligence, dazzling grades are probably not the determining factor of who's on top of the popularity pile at your students' school. Often it's not considered cool to be too smart until teenagers start approaching the later high school years. Even so, our society's value of intelligence is an important topic to approach during this session.

What isn't cool, of course, is appearing stupid in school. Dr. Dobson points out that "this feeling often begins during the very early school years, when they have trouble learning in school. Either they have a hard time learning to read, and they start worrying about this problem, or else they blurt out answers that cause everyone to laugh. They gradually start to believe that everybody . . . thinks they're stupid, and this brings the same old feelings of inferiority." Encourage your students by helping them realize that anyone who respects the Lord can be wise regardless of grades (Proverbs 1:7), and that the highest IQ in the world means nothing if it rejects God's wisdom (1 Corinthians 3:18-20).

Although their IQs are not yet highly valued by their peers, preteens' abilities and talents are held in awed esteem. It's the 13-year-old who can make an 18-footer in basketball or play the guitar like a superstar or win in gymnastics competition or perform incredible flips on a skateboard who gets noticed.

So it's quite a challenge to teach young adolescents the truth that God designed every wiggly preteen as His "workmanship" (the Greek word *poema*, from which we derive "poem," a work of art!), *created in Christ Jesus to do good works* (Ephesians 2:10). And *within that context*, even untalented, uncoordinated young people can claim with the apostle Paul, *I can do everything through him who gives me strength* (Philippians 4:13). Each person has enough talent and ability to do the will of the Lord!

Stuff

A third standard of importance in our culture is what we have, the things we can show off and brag about, the stuff we can afford. Needless to say, this standard of importance is often reinforced in the home, in the community and sometimes in the church itself. The grip of materialism on our culture is hard to shake—especially when you're a preteen who is made to feel inferior if you don't have much.

So don't try to change the materialistic course of our culture in this one segment of this one session in this one group of pre-adolescents. You won't have time!

Still, feel free to point out that God has other ideas about valuing possessions and money! For your own study, review the biblical truth that the real treasure of life, the quality that gives us true value, is knowing God. God's presence in us is like having glorious treasure in clay jugs (2 Corinthians 4:7). God promises that if we seek first His kingdom, He'll give us what we need (Matthew 6:25-33). The riches of our inheritance as God's children are really only seen when "the eyes of our hearts" are enlightened (Ephesians 1:18). Then we will realize the immeasurable, long-range value of having an intimate relationship with God rather than a huge store of possessions.

NOTE: This session can be an excellent time to offer to talk with any students who aren't sure about their relationship with the God who made them and values them so highly. See "Introducing Young People to Christ" (p. 117).

SESSION 2
TEACHING PLAN

APPROACH

Choose one Approach to direct the students' thinking about looks, brains and bucks.

APPROACH (5-7 minutes)

Materials needed: Paper and pencils.

The Contest. Instruct students to form groups of three or four. Give each group a sheet of paper and a pencil. Instruct students to draw a line down the center of the paper, title the left-hand column "The Guy" and the right-hand column "The Girl." Students work together to list the top three requirements for a winning contestant in "THE Guy and Girl of the Entire Hemisphere" contest. (There should be three requirements for the guy and three for the girl.)

Allow just 4-5 minutes for the listing; then rush around the room gathering up the lists from the groups. Announce that these are the qualifications for nominees for THE Guy and Girl of the Entire Hemisphere, then read the lists aloud. Pre-read each qualification before you announce it—there may be some gag listings!

Move into the Exploration by saying, **Your descriptions sound like people out of a magazine ad or a television commercial. They sound almost perfect. The fact is that none of us is qualified to be perfect. None of us can be all that advertising and other people say we should be. So we sometimes get depressed because we can't possibly measure up. We think that the only contest we'd be qualified to win is the Miss Freckle City or Mr. Blockhead Award. We have let the world tell us that the way God made us is not good enough. We believe that we have to be good-looking, have money, and have super-brains and abilities to be OK. However, in our session today we'll find out why God thinks each one of us is a special work of art!**

ALTERNATE APPROACH (5-7 minutes)

Materials needed: Scratch paper, pencils, chalkboard, chalk.

Teacher Preparation: Jot on the board: "Are you good-looking? Rich? Smart and talented?" Also, forewarn a "good sport" that you'll give him or her a bad time during this activity.

As students arrive, direct each to pick up paper and a pencil. Have students write "yes" at the top of one half of the paper and "no" at the top of the other side. Instruct students to individually ask everyone in the room the three questions: "Are you good-looking? Are you rich? Do you think you're smart or talented?" Students record the number of "yes" and "no" answers on their papers. After about three minutes, ask students to figure out the percentage of "no" answers they polled. Many will be generally confused, but allow the confusion for a few minutes. Act as if you're reviewing the forewarned Good Sport's percentages and say very loudly, **Oh, brother! Can't you figure this out? What's the matter, you flunk math in the fifth grade or something?** Activity will stop suddenly, at which time you explain that your prearranged insult is just an example of the way many people value something like brains—or good looks or money—over valuing the person God has made and loves. Move to the next part of the session by saying, **In our session today we'll look at what God says is valuable in a person.**

EXPLORATION

Use one of the Exploration suggestions to lead students in discovering what makes us feel superior or inferior to others.

EXPLORATION (45-50 minutes)

Materials needed: For each student—a Bible, a copy of "So What Makes You So Important, Eh?" Student Worksheet 4 and a pencil. For each group of four or five: A copy of "The Plain, Poor Ichabod and Dopey Desdemona Game" Student Worksheet 3 and a coin.

Step 1. Student Worksheet 3. Direct kids to form groups of four or five. Give each group a copy of Student Worksheet 3 and a coin. Instruct students to play game. To help make the instructions clear, give a few of your own examples. Allow about 10 minutes for play. Wrap up the game time by saying, **It's easy to see from this game, that comparing ourselves to others can cause feelings of inferiority. Now we're going to see that the most important thing is what God thinks about us.**

Step 2: Breakaway Bible Study. Distribute Bibles, pencils and copies of Student Worksheet 4.

Begin the study time by having students share answers to questions in the "Who Ya Gonna Believe?" section. Ask one or two volunteers to give evidence that their answers are correct. Have a race to look up and read Hebrews 6:18 to find evidence for the fact that God doesn't lie.

For the "What About Jesus?" segment, have students pair up. Pairs look up and match verses to state-

ments about Jesus. Ask, **Do you think Jesus would be popular according to the standards of our culture? Why or why not?**

Introduce the "What About You?" segment by saying, **We usually hear that if you're good-looking, rich, smart and talented, you're important. And we feel that if we don't measure up in some area we are not important. Now, either that's true or it isn't. We have learned that Jesus was not rich or "good-looking" by the world's standards, yet we know He is infinitely important! It seems as though God and society have different ideas about what makes a person important. Let's find out what the Bible says about your value.**

Direct each student to choose a spot in the room for a personal study time. Be available to help students complete worksheet as necessary.

Step 3: Wrap-Up. Reassemble students and ask volunteers to read their paraphrased verses. As you acknowledge the artistry of each paraphrase, add insights on these topics from your personal Bible study and this session's Teacher's Study.

Students can tape this worksheet near a mirror at home—it can be an "ad" on feeling good about themselves.

Be sure to mention that those who aren't sure God is their heavenly Father can talk with you after this session to make sure!

ALTERNATE EXPLORATION
(40-50 minutes)

Materials needed: Bibles, chalkboard and chalk, sheets of newsprint, felt pens, magazine advertisement.

Step 1: Show to the class a magazine advertisement that has an underlying message promising importance through buying some product. Write on the chalkboard: If you _____, you will be _____. Ask students to fill in the blanks to articulate the subtle message of the ad. (Example: If you buy Brand X jeans, you will be popular with the opposite sex.) Say, **Advertising in magazines and on TV has a big influence on us and on our society. How do ads affect us?** (We try to be like the people we see in the ads. We get depressed if we feel we don't measure up. We feel we aren't important.)

What if ads weren't trying to sell something but instead they were trying to help people see God's point of view? Today you're going to get a chance to make an ad telling about God's point of view.

Step 2: Ad-writing. Divide class into three groups. Give each group a Bible, a sheet of newsprint and a set of felt pens. Assign each group one of the following verses: Psalm 139:13,14; 1 Samuel 16:7; Ephesians 2:10. Each group looks up a verse and then creates a poster illustrating what God says about our bodies, our possessions or our abilities. Allow each group to present their "ad" and explain it to the others.

CONCLUSION

Choose one of the following concluding activities to reinforce the concept that we're important because of who we are in relation to God.

CONCLUSION *(5-7 minutes)*

Materials needed: Chalkboard and chalk or newsprint, tape and felt pen.

On the chalkboard or paper, draw the Canyon of Inferiority (see sketch).

As you draw, say, **On the road to adulthood each of you will pass through the teenage years. During those years you will be "walking" near a place called the Canyon of Inferiority. You don't have to fall**

into the canyon, but you might slip in to the outer rim at least a few times. How do you slip in? By comparing yourself to the image of the perfect girl or guy, seeing you don't measure up and feeling unimportant. What might help a person who is beginning to slip into the canyon? List students' ideas on the board (remember God's point of view, read Scriptures, pray for God's strength to resist the world's values, make a list of good things about him or herself, etc.). Tell students that the next session will give more ideas on ways to bypass this canyon.

Close in prayer, asking God to help students believe what *He* says about them. Thank Him for providing in the Bible the truth about ourselves.

ALTERNATE CONCLUSION
(5-7 minutes)

Materials needed: Two or three magazine ads that promise crazy results for those buying a particular product.

Teacher Preparation: Arrange for two or three of your natural actors to each read the wild promises of an ad.

Remind your students, **Teenagers often fall into the Canyon of Inferiority because they believe what society says—that looks, possessions and abilities make a person valuable. If they don't have these, teenagers start to feel inferior, even though they're not inferior at all!** Direct your actors to play "disc jockeys" by reading in funny voices the ads you've chosen. Say, **But today we discovered in the Bible that God says you are important regardless of your beauty, bucks or brains. And He never lies!** Close in a prayer of thanks for God's goodness and a plea for faith to believe what *He* says about us.

EXTRA FEATURES

Spice up your session with refreshments, a guest musician, crafts, crowdbreakers, games and worship:

Games—see page 15.
Snacks—see page 14.
Crafts—see page 15.

THE CANYON OF INFERIORITY: ALTERNATE ROUTE AHEAD

KEY VERSE

Humble yourselves therefore, under God's mighty hand, that he may lift you up in due time. Cast all your anxiety on him because he cares for you. 1 Peter 5:6,7

BIBLICAL BASIS

Exodus 4:10-14; Psalm 139:1-4,13-16; 2 Corinthians 12:7-10; James 1:2-4

PREPARING FOR ADOLESCENCE TEXT

Last section of chapter 1

FOCUS OF THE SESSION

With God's help, preteens deal with feelings of inferiority, changing what can be changed and accepting what cannot be changed.

AIMS OF THIS SESSION

During this session each learner will:

- DETERMINE his or her own susceptibility to the Canyon of Inferiority;
- FIND practical biblical solutions to common inferiority problems;
- COMMIT him or herself—flaws and all—to God

TEACHER'S STUDY

Basic Rx for Inferiority

Dr. Dobson, in *Preparing for Adolescence*, suggests to preteens who already feel inferior: "If you feel miserable about yourself and would like to escape somehow, to just run away from it all, or if you've been hurt when someone said unkind words, let me give you several suggestions that may help you." He then urges students to realize some basics:

- *They're not alone.* Most young people, even those who seem as if they haven't got a care in the world, have concerns that trouble them. Often they'll cover up those self-doubts by being shy, mean, silly or stuck-up. Dr. Dobson points out, "It will give you more confidence to know that everyone is afraid of embarrassment and ridicule."

- *God knows their hurts and concerns, and He cares.* Dobson's reminder of God's caring presence is for us adults too: "God sees you when you hurt. He knows those deep fears and frustrations that you thought no one understood. He knows the longings of your heart and He's always there during . . . those times when you feel totally alone."

- *They must face their problems.* Dobson suggests that students get alone to actually write out all the things they dislike about themselves. Your group will be doing this in your class session; but don't expect kids to make a full, honest list in that group setting. Dobson suggests that the student then check off the most serious problems he or she is feeling.

- *They need to find a true friend with whom to talk over these problems.* That mature confidante, of course, can be you! Dobson's advice to teenagers is, "Talk openly about your feelings, asking your friend to make suggestions about changing the things that concern you. It is very likely that many of the problems you face have been conquered by other people, and you may be able to profit from their experience."
- *With that friend's guidance, map a strategy to solve those problems.* In our last session, students touched on the fact that they are God's workmanship, created to do good works (see Ephesians 2:10). Trusting that fact, they can now take steps to avoid inferiority feelings that might inhibit them from fulfilling their God-given potential.

Solving the Unsolvable

Many of the problems that cause young people to feel inferior can't be erased through action plans. Dobson asks his readers, "But how will you handle the remaining items on your list that can't be changed? It would be wise to remember that the best way to have a healthy mind is to learn to accept the things which you cannot change."

On this point, be especially sensitive to any of your students who have some sort of physical handicap. As we saw last session, your students are immersed in a culture where physical appearance and abilities are right up at the top of the value scale; and handicapped students, those with physical handicaps and those with hearing aids or even glasses, sometimes feel the weight of inferiority much more acutely than other students. They especially can profit from this session and may want to talk further with you afterwards about how God can use this "thorn in the flesh" for something

good as He works out His plan for their lives.

The comforting thought that God knows our every concern (Psalm 139:1-4) is sometimes disturbing to young people when they begin to wonder why God doesn't do something about a problem they can't do anything about. Their conclusion often is that God must not really care if He knows all about this problem, but He won't pull off even the simplest miracle to remove it. You can teach your students that often God does not remove our flaws but uses them for His glory. In fact, God says, *My grace is sufficient for you, for my power is made perfect in weakness* (2 Corinthians 12:8).

Dobson reminds us that "God does not choose the superstars and the miracle men to do His work. All through the ages He has selected ordinary people with human flaws . . . to do His jobs."

Opportunity in Disguise

How can an unsolvable problem be handled, accepted, even greeted with an attitude of "counting it all joy"?

First, students can recognize that the presence of an unsolvable flaw can be an opportunity for God to use a person or teach a person in a unique way. Often God uses flaws and unsolvable problems in people's lives to teach them to rely on Him. People with unsolvable problems learn to relate to Him in ways they otherwise wouldn't.

Moses was an example of a man who had an inferiority complex—he described himself as "slow of speech and tongue." Dobson points out that *the Lord's anger burned against Moses* for using inferiority as an excuse for disobedience (Exodus 4:1-14). "You see," Dobson writes, "God intended to go with Moses and help him. That's why He didn't want Moses to hide behind an excuse of inferiority. The Lord doesn't want you to use this excuse of inferiority either, because He will help you accomplish what He tells you to do."

The apostle Paul's experience of a *thorn in the flesh*— possibly an eye problem—is a good New Testament example of God knowing and yet not removing a painful problem (see 2 Corinthians 12:7-10). Work to instill this possibly new thought into your students: Unlike the world's standard that says being flawless is the objective, God actually uses our flaws to cause us to become all that He wants us to be.

Compensation

Second, unsolvable problems force students to make up for those weaknesses by concentrating on strengths. Dobson suggests that preteens can balance those weak areas by excelling in some other areas.

"Not everybody can be the best-looking person in school. If this is your situation, say. 'All right, so what? There are a lot of other people in the same boat, and it doesn't really matter. My worth doesn't depend on the arrangement of my body. I'll put my effort into something that will help me feel good about myself. I'll be the best trumpet player in the band, or I'll succeed in my part-time job . . . or I'll make good grades in school, or I'll see how many friends I can make, or I'll learn how to play basketball as well as possible . . . or I'll just see how pleasant a personality I can develop . . . or I'll draw or paint or write poetry or short stories, or I'll become a good cook . . .' You can learn to make the most out of what you have, and that's the first step toward developing self-confidence and acceptance. So develop a skill that will make you proud of yourself, and gradually you will start to have a better self-concept. When you like yourself better, so will other people."

Having unsolvable flaws will force a person to develop skills that "flawless" superstars never learn. (For example, a person who isn't a natural athlete often learns a sport by working through the mechanics of specific movements. This type of person often makes a good coach, effectively teaching others.) As the trials of dealing with unsolvable problems test our faith in God's design, we can with James *consider it pure joy* that the process can result in a wonderful depth of maturity (see James 1:2-4). The alternative, of course, is to resent God's "flawed" design in our lives and allow a root of bitterness to grow up and cause trouble (see Hebrews 12:15).

Commitment

Third, students can take their worries about those unsolvable problems to God. Prayer is one practical action to release some of that worry (see Philippians 4:6,7). Another is an outright commitment of self—imperfections and all—to God for His use. In offering their bodies as *living sacrifices* to God (Romans 12:1), they'll enjoy the "grace" promised to the humble: *God opposes the proud but gives grace to the humble. Humble yourselves, therefore, under God's mighty hand, that he may lift you up in due time. Cast all your anxiety on him because he cares for you* (1 Peter 5:5-7). Dobson suggests that adolescents pray this prayer: "Dear Jesus, I want Your will for my life, not because I'm a superstar or superman or superwoman, but because You promised to help those who admit their weaknesses. I'm depending on Your power and Your strength to make something beautiful out of my life."

SESSION 3 TEACHING PLAN

APPROACH

Choose one Approach to direct the students' thinking about the alternate route—around the Canyon of Inferiority.

APPROACH *(5-7 minutes)*

Materials needed: Copy for each student of the "Suspect Signs" Student Worksheet 5, pencils.

Distribute worksheets and pencils. Say, **Along the road to "Adultsville" there will be lots of "signs." If you believe what some of the signs say and follow their directions you may end up in the Canyon of Inferiority, feeling bad about yourself.** Volunteers read road signs aloud to class. Students circle one of the road signs they would be most likely to believe. Volunteers share answers. Say, **We know that each of us is a special creation of God, but we still feel inferior sometimes. In today's session you'll learn some practical steps to take when you're feeling inferior.**

ALTERNATE APPROACH *(5-7 minutes)*

Materials needed: Chalkboard and chalk.

Use chalk and chalkboard to illustrate the following brainteaser as you explain it to your students (see sketch).

Say, **Imagine that you are traveling through Bunga-bungaland on your way to Adultsville. You have a wolf, a chicken and a sack of grain that you are taking with you. You come to a river that you must cross. Your canoe is only large enough to hold you and one other thing. You need to use the canoe to get yourself, the grain, the chicken and the wolf across the river. The problem is that if left alone, the chicken will eat the grain and if left alone, the wolf will eat the chicken.** Ask students for suggestions on how to solve the problem. Illustrate their suggestions on the chalkboard to see if they work. After about four minutes, give the solution: Take the chicken across; then come back and take the grain across. Leave the grain on the other side and bring the chicken back with you so it won't eat the grain. Leave the chicken on this side and take the wolf across. Then come back for the chicken. It's just that simple!

Relate the solving of this puzzle to today's aims. Say, **Sometimes during your teenage years, you may feel as if there's no way out of bad feelings, of feeling inferior. Solving our brainteaser took some thoughtful planning. In a similar way, the problems of the Canyon of Inferiority can be handled. We're going to look at some ways right now.**

EXPLORATION

Use one of the Exploration suggestions to lead students in understanding ways to face inferiority problems with action.

EXPLORATION *(50-60 minutes)*

Materials needed: Bibles, copy for each student of "Good Ideas for When You Feel Bad About Yourself" Student Worksheets 6 and 7 and "Dr. Schnoffogian's. . ." Student Worksheet 8, pencils, one or two staplers.

Teacher Preparation: Fold a copy of worksheets 6 and 7 on the dotted lines, first horizontally, then vertically. With worksheet 6 on the outside, staple both worksheets together to form a booklet (see sketch on next page). Invite and orient a guest to play the role of a counseling client in *Step 2* of this activity.

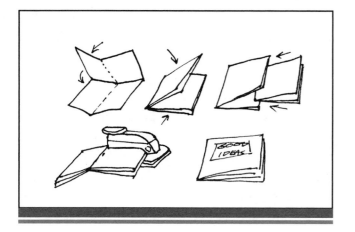

Step 1: "Good Ideas . . ." booklet. Distribute Bibles, pencils, staplers and Student Worksheets 6 and 7. Instruct students to make booklets. Ask students who finish first to look up the Bible verses in their booklets and be ready to read them aloud in a few minutes.

Say, **This booklet is full of good ideas to help you when you're feeling bad about yourself. Following these suggestions can help you avoid slipping into the Canyon of Inferiority.** Instruct students to follow along and fill in the blanks as you read through the booklet together. Humor may help students become more verbal about a subject that teenagers often take too seriously, making it seem worse than it is.

Step 2: Introduce the following activity with some psuedo-scientific puffery such as, **Thank you very much, distinguished psychiatrists and psychologists, for joining us in this very, very significant practicum in psychoanalyzing the ramifications of the teenage inferiority complex. You will be advising a client on his or her inferiority problems in the area of looks, brains or bucks. You will have 15 minutes to prepare your prognosis and advice for this client.**

At this point have your "client" enter the room. She should introduce herself and describe the inferiority feelings she's been having in the areas of looks, bucks and brains. This monologue should be brief and humorous. Example: "Thanks for inviting me to visit your class. I almost didn't come though. I'm sure no one will like me. It's my hair. It's the wrong color. It's too curly and it's ugly and that's one reason no one

likes me. And I don't have enough money for a good haircut . . ."

Divide class into three counseling groups: one group counseling about looks; one about possessions; one about brains or talents. Give each group a copy of the Student Worksheet 8. Using their "Good Ideas..." booklets, each group plans a way to counsel the client regarding the group's assigned problem area. A volunteer from each group records the group's ideas on the "Dr. Schnoffle's . . ." worksheet.

Be available to help each group work through its worksheet, realizing that they'll hardly scratch the surface of possible solutions.

Step 3: After the allotted 15 minutes, have the groups take turns sitting in a circle around the client, counseling her as she role-plays a teenager who has inferiority feelings about looks, possessions and abilities. Limit each group's counseling session to five minutes. Say, **We can deal with inferiority feelings as we work to change what we can and with God's help handle what we can't change.**

ALTERNATE EXPLORATION
(50-55 minutes)

Materials needed: Bibles, copy for each student of the "Good Ideas . . ." Student Worksheets 6 and 7 and the "Dear Gabby" Student Worksheet 9, pencils and staplers.

Teacher Preparation: Using worksheets 6 and 7, prepare a sample booklet as directed in the original Exploration.

Step 1: Dear Gabby. **One of the first steps toward avoiding inferiority feelings is to write out the things that bother you about yourself. Take a few minutes now to write a note to the famous advice columnist Dear Gabby. You can write honestly about yourself or make up a problem. It may be something about your body, how rich or poor you are, how smart or talented you are or something else. Be very specific about what that problem is.** As you distribute Student Worksheets 9, say, **Don't put your name on the paper, and you can disguise your handwriting so that no one will ever know who wrote the problem. Sign it with a silly name**

like Hopeless Harvey or Lame Brain Laroo.

When students are finished they fold their papers and place them in a pile.

Step 2: "Good Ideas . . ." booklet. Same as *Step 1* of original Exploration.

Step 3: Gabby's Advice. Shuffle "Dear Gabby" letters and distribute one to each student. No one should have his or her own paper. Students now use information from "Good Ideas . . ." booklet to write a helpful response to the person with a problem. When students are finished, volunteers read several Dear Gabby problems and responses. Sum up this Exploration with the thought that we can deal with inferiority feelings as we work to change what we can and with God's help handle or accept what we can't change.

CONCLUSION

Choose one of the following activities to help kids understand that God didn't design them to feel inferior but to feel excited about how they can be used by Him.

CONCLUSION *(12-15 minutes)*

Materials needed: Scratch paper, pencils, a metal trash can and matches.

Teacher Preparation: Review the sample prayer of commitment at the end of this session's Teacher's Study. Obtain permission from the proper board, group or committees for your group to burn papers outside in a consecration ceremony.

Challenge your students with: (1) God knows all about the problems that get you down; He made you. (2) Get help to change what you can change; pray that you'll grow to accept what you can't change. (3) God has big plans for you that can't be accomplished with-out His help. He designed you to need Him! (4) Don't excuse yourself because you've got some imperfections you can't change. (5) Concentrate on your strengths; make the most of what you have. Then take your worries about those unchangeable problems to God in prayer.

The Commitment Service. Direct students to write on a piece of paper problems that are or seem now to be unchangeable. Have them crumple these sheets. Lead students in prayer as they bow and consider committing their problems and feelings of inferiority to God. Say, **God created each of us with good qualities and He wants to use each of us as part of His plan for the world. As we give ourselves to God, He will help us overcome our problems and show us ways that we can help others. Let's always remember this time when we symbolically gave ourselves—problems and all—back to the God who made us!** Together toss your crumpled papers into the fire.

ALTERNATE CONCLUSION
(2-3 minutes)

Materials needed: Scratch paper, pencils.

Prayer of Commitment. Direct students to write on a scrap of paper their unchangeable flaws and problems. Allowing them to pray silently, lead them phrase by phrase through a prayer of commitment such as the one at the end of this session's Teacher's Study. Suggest, as in the above Conclusion activity, that God wants to use each of us to help His kingdom grow and He wants to keep us from going over the edge of that Canyon of Inferiority. Encourage students to keep their unchangeable problem lists as a reminder to rely on Him and so to conquer those feelings of inferiority!

EVERYBODY'S DOING IT

KEY VERSE

Do not conform any longer to the pattern of this world, but be transformed by the renewing of your mind. Romans 12:2

BIBLICAL BASIS

Matthew 26:69-75; Acts 4:18-20; 7:58—8:1; 14:19; Romans 1:16; 12:1,2; 2 Corinthians 4:16-18; 2 Timothy 1:7

PREPARING FOR ADOLESCENCE TEXT

Chapter 2

FOCUS OF THE SESSION

Renewed thinking and courage from God's Spirit can help adolescents resist pressure to conform.

AIMS OF THIS SESSION

During this session each learner will:

- GIVE biblical examples of conforming and of resisting conformity;
- DISCUSS ways people his or her age are pressured to conform;
- PLAN responses to the inevitable pressures to conform.

TEACHER'S STUDY

This is a particularly important session for which you need to remember your own teenage experiences. How old were you when you first felt pressured to do something you knew was wrong? Undoubtedly it was long before your teenage years. Spend some time remembering those feelings—the pressure, the fear, the regret when you gave in. Bring your musing up to the present: In what ways are you now pressured to conform to world-system actions and attitudes? Do you give in? Why or why not? This kind of self-evaluation will prompt you to pray more specifically for your students and to lead this session with the conviction that what they learn now about resisting world-system peer pressure will last them a lifetime.

Conforming

Conformity isn't all bad, of course. When you bathe, pay taxes and say "Good morning," you're conforming to the actions of millions of others. Likewise, peer pressure is often a positive influence on teenagers. For example, in a group of outgoing friends, a shy teenager may learn to share openly. So avoid the extreme of announcing that it's always wrong to conform to the actions of a non-Christian.

In this session we are concerned with conformity that has destructive results. Dr. Dobson says a conformist "is someone who is afraid to be different from the majority; he feels a great need to be like everyone else."

A teenager with feelings of inferiority, who is afraid of ridicule, is likely to succumb to the pressure to conform. A teenager may participate in activities that are destructive or against his or her own better judgment in order to fit in and avoid ridicule. This is destructive conformity. Even going along with the crowd on issues that involve personal preferences rather than morals can be destructive. And this going along only reinforces the person's original feelings that he or she is inferior, that his or her ideas or abilities aren't as acceptable as the crowd's.

For example, a 13-year-old guy who feels insecure about his "manhood" is afraid to admit he loves to sew since most of the other guys will ridicule him. When he gives in to the pressure to always talk about motorcycles and sports, he has to fake interest. He therefore wonders whether he's much of a man at all since no other guys seem interested in sewing. The outcome? His original inferiority is confirmed, and he continues the conformity spiral right over the edge of the old Canyon of Inferiority!

Classroom Conformity

Dr. Dobson calls this form of conformity destructive—even though it doesn't involve wrong actions. He describes an experiment in which a class of teenagers was told they would be tested on how well they could see from their position in the room. The test administrator held up a card and asked the group which of three lines on the card was the longest. The administrator would point to each of the three lines on the card, and the students were to raise their hands when the longest line on the card was indicated. What one of the students didn't know, of course, was that the rest of the class was clued in beforehand to raise their hands at the second longest line. Each time a new card was introduced, the instructor repeated that they were to choose the longest line. He would point to the shortest, then the second longest—and, dead-panned, the class would raise hands. The test subject, Dobson says, would invariably "look around in disbelief. It was obvious that Line B was the longest line, but everybody seemed to think Line A was longer. [The subject] later admitted that he thought, 'I must not have been listening during the directions. I'd better do what everybody else is doing or they'll laugh at me.'"

In the testing, only 25 percent of the young people would go against the crowd even though they knew the crowd was mistaken. That is, an average of three-fourths of the students in your group will probably give in to excessive conformity even when they're convinced the crowd is wrong.

Dobson writes about another interesting characteristic revealed in the peer pressure study. "If just one other student recognized (voted for) the right line, then the chances were greatly improved that the fellow who was being studied would also do what he thought was right." In other words having even one friend who is willing to "go against the flow" greatly increases a person's likelihood of doing what he thinks is right in spite of peer pressure.

This is probably a good time to evaluate your own battles with teenage peer pressure and to assess your strength against the crowd both then and now. The not-so-obvious point of the second experiment Dobson cited is that being that one lone hand who will go against a mistaken crowd is exactly what the crowd needs. God can use peer pressure situations to develop our confidence and ability to live by our convictions. When a teenager stands alone for his or her convictions in a classroom of peers, leadership training is taking place.

Can You Say No?

Teenagers who feel inferior and insecure are especially vulnerable to peer pressure. Following the crowd seems to offer a chance to "fit in" and feel good about oneself. Imagine the boy who is socially awkward and has always longed to be "one of the guys." He attends a party and is offered a marijuana cigarette by one of the boys he admires. Even though he doesn't *want* to smoke it and feels it's wrong, it may be hard to pass up what appears to be a coveted gesture of friendship from a member of the "in" crowd.

Pressure to conform to what is wrong exploits feelings of inferiority and fear. For example, a teenage girl who feels insecure about her physical appearance fears rejection by boys if she doesn't go along with the crowd's pressure to be sexually active. When she does attract boys because of her promiscuity, she worries that they don't really care about her as a person—which deepens her feelings of inferiority!

Dobson says that this pressure to conform "explains the most important reason why drugs are being used by teenagers every day throughout this country." He wishes that every teenager would be primed to respond to destructive peer pressure. When offered drugs, cigarettes, alcohol or sexual promiscuity, a teenager can answer with courage, "Why should I wreck my body? It's the only one I have! If you guys want to do something crazy, go ahead. But I think it's stupid!" Dobson points out that displaying confidence when the pressure is greatest is a key sign of growing up. He also notes that most teenagers respect a peer who has the courage to be his or her own person even when being mocked and teased. "An individual with this kind of confidence," writes Dobson, "often becomes a leader. He has shown that he doesn't feel as inferior as the other followers. . . . He's likely to influence others who are looking for that one friend who will increase their confidence."

Peter and Paul

Two biblical characters who were influenced by peer pressure are the apostles Peter and Paul. Read through Peter's denial of Christ (Matthew 26:69-75) and work at sensing the emotional pressures in this familiar story. What was the crowd's "message"? What factors were involved in Peter's decision to lie? You won't need to examine the psychoanalytic background of Peter's actions to convey the story's import to your students: Even Bible bigwigs were influenced by peer pressure.

The apostle Paul's pre-conversion experience with conformity is also something your kids may identify with. Think through Paul's (Saul's) conformity as he stood and watched the coats of those stoning Stephen (Acts 7:58—8:1). Notice especially that Saul, although not throwing stones himself, was "giving approval to (Stephen's) death." Student Worksheet 10 asks a question that you yourself can ponder: When was the last time you went along with the wrong actions of the crowd—although you didn't really participate yourself?

The New Testament documents the radical changes God's Spirit brought about in Peter's and Paul's characters. They became "new creations" (2 Corinthians 5:17), even in their responses to conform to the crowd. Read through Peter's new response to pressure (Acts 4:18-20), as well as Paul's (Acts 14:19,20; Romans 1:16; 2 Corinthians 4:16-18). What made the difference? They knew conformity was wrong, planned to resist conformity and had the courage to stand for what was right.

Preparing for Tough Spots

Christian adolescents need special training to resist destructive conformity. Encourage your students to be prepared for pressure. Think through the tough spots your kids will consider on the Student Worksheet 11 in this session. Help them think of creative ways to respond to these inevitable pressures to conform.

Your students don't have to flounder against the tide of peer pressure by themselves. The New Testament points out at least two steps to help them overcome destructive conformity to the world system.

Step 1: Renew your thinking according to God's Word. Nonconformity demands a new way of thinking—thinking the way God thinks. King David advised that a person will be blessed if he or she doesn't walk *in the counsel of the wicked . . . but his [or her] delight is in the law of the Lord* (see Psalm 1:1,2). "Marching to a different drummer" requires a new wisdom based on God's thinking. So encourage your students to study and memorize Scripture to help them resist the crowd.

Step 2: Rely on God's Spirit for courage. Paul writes to timid Timothy, *God did not give us a spirit of timidity, but a spirit of power, of love and of self-discipline* (2 Timothy 1:7). Train your students to pray for power in tough peer pressure situations.

Putting into practice these concepts of renewed thinking and relying on God's Spirit will help your students develop into powerful, loving and self-disciplined leaders.

SESSION 4 TEACHING PLAN

APPROACH

Choose one Approach to direct your students' thinking about conforming because of fear of what others will say.

APPROACH (5-7 minutes)

Materials needed: A small grouping of five chairs positioned at the front of the room, strip of white cloth, a crutch.

Teacher Preparation: Well before the session, prepare your best boy "actor" to play the part of The Conformist. As students arrive, quickly select a cast of five others. Each will display a funny quirk or habit: • One taps foot constantly. • One twirls her/his hair around all the time. • One continually checks self in mirror. • One constantly mumbles "Hum, hum, hum" between phrases. • One has a bandaged head and a crutch.

Group Therapy Skit. As your session starts, The Conformist comes in and asks you where the waiting room is for the good Dr. Schnoffle. You ask him, "What's your problem?" He says, "I'm a conformist. I do everything everybody around me does." Point him to a group of chairs at the front of the room.

As each new patient arrives, The Conformist looks at him or her and gradually starts doing the same motions. The characters may ad lib conversation if they like. When The Conformist is thrashing around doing all the motions at once, the last patient arrives—the injured person. The Conformist screams, "No! No!" and runs out the door.

Applaud as you take the floor, explaining that conforming—doing things others do—can wear you out and can be dangerous. **Doing what the crowd does is not necessarily wrong. But if what the crowd is doing goes against what God teaches in the Bible, then conformity is wrong. We all feel pressured to conform at times. Today we'll find out that even Bible bigwigs felt the pressure.**

ALTERNATE APPROACH (5-7 minutes)

Materials needed: Chalk and chalkboard.

Conformity Poll. Ask the group what things are "in" these days (music groups to listen to, shoes to wear, brands of clothing, activities to be into, etc.). List these on the chalkboard. Then instruct each student to pick one of these activities or items—one he or she is into—and in 60 seconds find out how many others in the room have that item or practice that activity. Call a definite "Stop" to the minute-long poll. Have students return to their seats and ask, **Is there anything wrong with having things or doing things others have and do?** Allow students to respond. Then say, **Doing what the crowd does is not necessarily wrong. But if what the crowd is doing goes against what God teaches in the Bible, then conformity is wrong. We all feel pressured to conform at times. Today we'll look at two Bible characters who were influenced by peer pressure.**

EXPLORATION

Use one of the following Explorations to lead your students in discovering ways to handle pressures to conform.

EXPLORATION (45-50 minutes)

Materials needed: For each student—Bible, copy of "Even Bible Bigwigs" Student Worksheet 10, pencil.

Teacher Preparation: Invite two adults or older teenagers to present Peter's and Paul's experiences of the pressure to conform. Each should dress in a Bible-era costume and tell his story as a contemporary event.

Step 1: Guests. Introduce your two invited guests—two of the most influential people in the New Testament: Peter and Paul. Each character should take about five minutes to dramatize as colorfully as possible his story as outlined in the Bible passages listed on worksheet. Both should emphasize:

• that knowing God's Word is essential to knowing when conforming is OK and when it's not; and

• that the courage it takes to go against pressure makes you into a leader.

Step 2: Student Worksheet 10. Distribute Bibles, worksheets and pencils. Students work to fill in worksheets, referring to Scripture passages when necessary. Be available to assist students who need help.

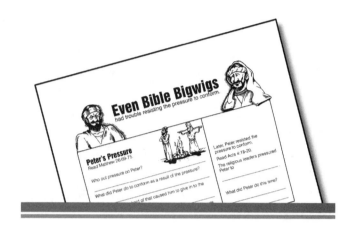

Step 3: Pep Talk. Hold an open Bible. Use insights from your own Bible study and this session's Teacher's Study as you give a brief pep talk on:

• Romans 12:2. Note the key words—"conform," "world," "renewing."
• 2 Timothy 1:7. Emphasize the need to depend on God's Spirit to handle the fear, the timidity of conformity. Remind students of the interplay of fear, inferiority and conforming as suggested in this session's Teacher's Study.

Wrap up this segment by asking, **Is it wrong to want to be like others? To have things they have? I mean, if everyone is riding mountain bikes, is it wrong to ride one, too? Conforming to the crowd is only wrong if what the crowd is doing is wrong. But if the action isn't wrong, conforming just takes a lot of time, energy and money that you might spend in more satisfying ways. For example, have you ever worked really hard to get something like the right style athletic shoe, only to get a pair and not feel any better about life anyway?**

ALTERNATE EXPLORATION
(40-45 minutes)

Materials needed: For each student—Bible, a copy of "Even Bible Bigwigs" Student Worksheet 10, pencil.

Step 1: Paired Bible Study. Pass out Bibles, Student Worksheets and pencils. Divide the group into pairs who may choose to study either Peter's or Paul's experiences with conformity. Early finishers may go on and study the other Bible character's experience. Ask volunteers for reports on the study.

Step 2: "What If?" Skits. Divide class into two groups. Assign one group to come up with a skit portraying what might have happened if Peter had not lied. Assign the other group to create a skit about what might have happened if Paul had tried to stop the stoning of Stephen.

Have groups perform skits. Say, **We can't *know* what would have happened if Paul or Peter had stood up for what was right. But we know one thing—it isn't easy to go against the crowd.**

Step 3: Same as *Step 3* of original Exploration.

CONCLUSION

Use one of the Conclusions to help each student plan responses to the inevitable pressures to conform.

CONCLUSION *(15-20 minutes)*

Materials needed: A copy for each student of "Tough Spots" Student Worksheet 11, pencils.

Tough-spot Role-play. Distribute the Student Worksheets and pencils. Rearrange class into groups of three or four. Assign each group one "pressure" from the worksheet. Groups role-play a situation in which one student encounters the pressure to conform and shows how he or she might handle the pressure.

As each group role-plays, other students write on worksheet ways to resist that temptation.

Have students take a moment on their own to complete the "Your Plan" section of the worksheet. Have students keep tabs on the pressures they're now facing. Suggest that taking more notice of those pressure attacks will help them resist the temptation to conform.

Close by praying for each student by name. Pray that each student will be courageous in standing for what's right, even against the pressure of the crowd.

ALTERNATE CONCLUSION
(7-10 minutes)

Materials needed: Bibles, index cards, scratch paper, pencils.

Divide class into two groups. Give each group a piece of paper and a pencil. Groups compete to see who can come up with the longest list of ways teen-

agers are pressured to conform. After two minutes, collect lists. Briefly discuss lists with class by asking, **What do you think is the most difficult pressure to resist? Which pressure to conform do you feel is destructive? What are some ways to resist the pressure to conform?**

Personalized Verse. Instruct students to read 2 Timothy 1:7 and write out a personalized version of the verse on an index card. Example: God did *not give* **Lauren** *a spirit of timidity* **when she feels pressured to drink alcohol,** *but a spirit of power, of love and of self-discipline.* You may want to write several examples on the chalkboard. Encourage students to tape this message up in their room or school locker. It can be a reminder not to conform to what's wrong.

In closing, pray for each student by name, that each would rely on God's Spirit to be courageous in resisting destructive conformity.

EXTRA FEATURES

Add one or more of these features to your session to increase friendship and impact:

Games—see page 15.
Snacks—see page 14.
Crafts—see page 15.

SOMETHING CRAZY IS HAPPENING TO MY BODY!

KEY VERSE
I praise you because I am fearfully and wonderfully made; your works are wonderful, I know that full well.
Psalm 139:14

BIBLICAL BASIS
Genesis 1:27,28; Psalm 139:13-16; 1 Corinthians 6:18,19;
Ephesians 5:31; 1 Thessalonians 4:3-8; Hebrews 13:4

PREPARING FOR ADOLESCENCE TEXT
Chapter 3

FOCUS ON THE SESSION
An understanding of adolescent sexual development and the responsibilities it brings can help teenagers fulfill God's plan for their bodies.

AIMS OF THIS SESSION
During this session, each learner will:

- READ in the Bible God's plan for human sexuality;
- DISCUSS common concerns about adolescent sexuality;
- PRAY a prayer of commitment to honor God with his or her body.

TEACHER'S STUDY

This session provides a unique opportunity for you to present the subject of sexuality to your students in the light of God's Word. The session provides two possible emphases. You may choose to concentrate more heavily on the biological aspect of sexual development or on the psychological and spiritual aspects, depending on the needs of your students and your own unique skills as a teacher. For this session you may want to consider:

- Inviting a qualified guest (doctor, nurse, counselor, teacher or minister) to lead the discussion about sexuality;

- Informing parents about the content of this session well in advance and getting permission for each student's attendance using the permission letter provided in the reproducible section of this book.

Review this Teacher's Study as background information for your upcoming session. It serves as a syllabus for a talk on physical and sexual development in adolescents.

Time to Grow Up
If you're a little nervous about tackling this session, try to focus on your student's needs rather than

your nerves! Physical changes can be frightening to young people unless those changes are expected and looked forward to as blessings. Many young teenagers have a surprising lack of knowledge about physical growth and sexual development; and this ignorance can result in everything from experimental sexual relationships to years of ungrounded fears. Your students deserve simple, clear instruction in this area. So share the following insights from Dr. Dobson's book:

The pituitary gland starts and controls the growing-up process. This master gland sends out chemicals called hormones to say, "It's time to grow up." Some of those hormones determine when your body will reach puberty.

Puberty is when the body begins to change in order to prepare itself for parenthood. Puberty usually includes:

- Rapid growth spurts.
- Skin changes. These occur in both boys and girls and often cause much distress. Solutions:

  1. Keep the skin clean. Wash several times a day.
  2. Eat a balanced diet, avoiding fatty foods and sweets.
  3. If the skin problem gets serious, ask to be taken to a dermatologist.

- Fatigue. Expect to be unusually tired at times. A teenager needs more rest than a nine- or ten-year-old.

When boys become men, muscles become stronger, and their movement is better coordinated. Body size will increase. Body hairs will appear on the face, under the arms and in the pubic area around the sex organs. The sex organs will enlarge.

Voice changes happen very quickly. The voice may squeak or crack for a few months or years. Boys sometimes have nocturnal emissions or "wet dreams." A fluid called semen comes from a boy's penis at night. This nocturnal emission is the body's way of discharging the extra semen in a maturing boy.

When a girl becomes a woman, her body will become more rounded and curvy. Her breasts will enlarge and may sometimes become sore. The soreness just signals change. Hair will grow under a girl's arms, on her legs and in the pubic region.

Menstruation

Both boys and girls need to understand the process of menstruation. About once a month a woman's body prepares itself to be able to have a baby. One of the ways the body prepares itself is by lining the walls of the uterus with blood. If a woman has sexual intercourse and becomes pregnant (we'll talk more about how this occurs later), the baby will begin to grow inside the woman's body, in the uterus. The blood which lines the uterus nourishes and protects the baby.

If the woman does not have intercourse and become pregnant, the blood lining the uterus is not needed and will be discharged each month through an opening in the woman's body called the vagina. This is the same opening through which babies are born. The discharge lasts from three to seven days. During this time a woman needs to wear a special pad to absorb the blood and protect her clothing. Menstruation may begin as early as nine or ten years or as late as sixteen or seventeen.

If a girl has menstrual pain or is worried about this process, she should immediately talk to her mother, doctor, or a close adult friend.

The menstruation process is normal. It's a sign that a girl is becoming a woman. God planned for menstruation to be a part of growing up.

Sexuality

Sexual drives will become more and more prominent as the teenage years pass. Older youth will want to spend more time with the opposite sex. Boys will become very interested in the bodies of girls. Girls are not quite so attracted to a boy's body, but they will be more fascinated by the boy himself—in the way he walks, talks and thinks. Girls will often get crushes on one boy after another.

Masturbation is the act of rubbing your own sex organs to get a pleasurable feeling as in intercourse. Most boys do this at some time during adolescence, and so do many girls.

There are many scary stories about the effects of practicing masturbation. Some people say it will make you crazy. Or it will make you sick or weak. None of these stories is true. Christians have different opinions about how God views this act. The Bible is silent on this point. Many Christian counselors reassure teenagers with the opinion that masturbation isn't much of an issue with God. It's a normal part of adolescence which involves no one else. Dr. Dobson says, "I'm not telling you to masturbate, and I hope you won't feel the need for it. But if you do, it is my opinion that you should not struggle with guilt over it. I suggest you talk with God personally about this matter and decide what He wants you to do."

Sexual intercourse is a special way God designed for a man and woman who are married to express their love for one another, to bring each other pleasure and to have children. It is a very satisfying experience, which husbands and wives do regularly.

During sexual intercourse a fluid comes out of the man's penis and enters the woman's body. This fluid contains sperm cells. Sometimes one of the sperm cells combines with one of the woman's eggs cells and a new life begins. The woman is now pregnant and a baby will begin to develop inside the woman's uterus. Near the end of nine months, the mother's body will push the baby out into its new world.

The appetite for sex is something God created within people. Sex is not dirty and it is not evil. The desire for sex was God's idea—not ours. It's a wonderful, beautiful mechanism, no matter what some people may have said about it. But God intends for us to be in control of the desire for sexual intercourse. God has stated repeatedly in the Bible that each person is to save his or her body for the person he or she will eventually marry, and that it is wrong to satisfy an appetite for sex with a boy or girl before we get married. It's a good idea for young people to decide early on to save their bodies for their marriage partners.

Sex before marriage can have various consequences:

- Sexually Transmitted Diseases (STDs) are caused by having sexual intercourse with someone who has the disease. Chlamydia, syphilis, gonorrhea, herpes and AIDS are widespread today and can have a damaging effect on the body if they are untreated. AIDS causes death.
- Another consequence of having sex before marriage may be an unwanted baby. God intended a child to have both a loving mother and father in a stable home. When an unmarried girl becomes pregnant, the couple or often just the girl is forced to choose from options which have profound and painful effects on the parents and child. These options include giving a child up for adoption, raising a child without being emotionally or financially prepared, and abortion.
- Emotional pain and stress is another result of premarital sex. Physical intimacy was meant to be experienced within the safety of a committed marriage relationship. When a couple who has been intimate breaks up, there is pain and grief. These hurts complicate subsequent relationships.
- Premarital sex is sin, and sin separates us from God's fellowship. Christian teenagers who are involved in sexual relationships find that they no longer are growing in Christian maturity. Their sexual relationships have become more important than their relationship with God.

Teenagers who make a commitment to wait until marriage to have sex may experience some temporary "negative consequences" such as social pressure and delayed gratification. But this decision will contribute to the experience of many positive consequences such as:

- growth in Christian maturity and self-control;
- security and trust in the love of his or her partner;
- sex without guilt or emotions complicated by past relationships;
- sex without fear of disease;
- ability to provide a stable home for children.

Dr. Dobson closes this section of *Preparing for Adolescence* with a message to youth: "Nearly everyone growing up in our culture worries and frets over the subject of sex. I want to help you avoid those anxieties. Your sexual development is a normal event that is being controlled inside your body. It will work out all right, so you can just relax and let it happen. However, you will have to control your sexual desires in the years ahead, and that will require determination and will power. But if you can learn to channel your sexual impulses the way God intended, this part of your nature can be one of the most fascinating and wonderful aspects of your life."

SESSION 5
TEACHING PLAN

APPROACH

NOTE: This session is unique in that it contains two separate tracks. The original Approach, Exploration and Conclusion deal mainly with the biology of sexual development. The Alternate Approach, Exploration and Conclusion deal with the psychological and spiritual aspects of teenage sexuality. These activities are not interchangeable as in other sessions. Choose the track that will best meet the needs of your students.

APPROACH (5-7 minutes)

Materials needed: For each student—a copy of the "Spring Fling" Student Worksheet 12, pencils, shoe box, scissors.

Teacher Preparation: Cut a slit in the lid of the shoe box.

Distribute worksheets and pencils. Instruct students to read worksheets and then write a question they have about sexual development. Students should place folded worksheets in shoe box. The Exploration leader will attempt to answer these questions as part of his or her lecture. Say, **It's natural for young people to have lots of questions about sex. Today we'll try to answer some of those questions and find out what the Bible says about it.**

ALTERNATE APPROACH (5-7 minutes)

Materials needed: Seven pieces of poster board, yarn, tape, different colored felt pens, scissors.

Teacher Preparation: On each piece of poster board letter the following words: "sex," "pregnancy," "dating," "love," "commitment," "companionship," "God." Use yarn and tape to hang each sign from the ceiling.

As students arrive, say, **The words you see hanging in our classroom are topics that can be of concern to teenagers. Which word do you think describes what is most important to teenage girls in a dating relationship? Teenage boys?** Allow students to answer. Discuss each of the words as it relates

to teenagers. Say, **Sex is an issue you will face as you get older, so it's important to know what God says about it. Today we'll look at some Bible passages about sex.**

EXPLORATION

Use the Exploration to instruct students about the physical changes they can expect during their teenage years. Use the Alternate Exploration to emphasize the spiritual and psychological aspects of sexual relationships.

EXPLORATION (40-50 minutes)

Materials needed: A copy of the "Body Talk" Student Worksheet 13 for each student, pencils, poster board, colored felt pens.

Teacher Preparation: Optional: Arrange for a woman to lead a girls' group and a man to lead a boys' group. Leaders might be pastors, Christian medical doctors or nurses, Christian counselors, teachers or other concerned adults who are willing to prepare for this teaching session. You may have a unique opportunity as a group leader to have an open discussion with students with whom you already have a close relationship.

Using various colored felt pens, letter the words of Psalm 139:14 on a large sheet of poster board. Have group leaders review the Teacher's Study material, read chapter 3 in *Preparing for Adolescence* and become familiar with the "Body Talk" Student Worksheet students will be completing during the session.

Step 1: Introduce group leader and pass out worksheet and pencils. Leader lectures group on the content of the Teacher's Study and worksheet. Instruct students to put check by each topic as it is discussed. After each topic, leader should pause to allow students to cross out the statements that are untrue for that topic. Make sure the lecturer attempts to answer students' written questions from Approach activity.

Step 2: Say, **You have learned some amazing things about the way God designed your bodies. He doesn't want us to feel afraid or confused about the way He has made us. In fact He wants us to praise Him for His wonderful work!** Show colorful poster of the words to Psalm 139:14. Read it together with students. Lead students in a brief prayer in which they consider the amazing way in which they were made and silently pray the words of Psalm 139:14.

ALTERNATE EXPLORATION
(50-60 minutes)

Materials needed: Bibles, copy for every two students of "Sam and Tonya" and "Rachel and Alex" Student Worksheets 14 and 15, copy for each student of "John and Kirsten" Student Worksheet 16, paper, pencils, chalk, chalkboard.

Teacher Preparation: Letter the following Bible references on the chalkboard: Genesis 2:20-25; Ephesians 5:31; 1 Thessalonians 4:3-8; Hebrews 13:4.

Step 1: The Bible Speaks. Say, **As you know, dur-** **ing your teen years your bodies go through changes. Your bodies are developing sexually. You are becoming adults. You will have the ability to form intimate relationships with the opposite sex, and eventually become parents. Your sexuality is a good important part of your life. Since it is so important, we want to take a look at what the Bible says about sexuality and how you can please God in this area of your lives.** Divide class into four groups. Distribute Bibles, paper and pencils. Assign each group to look up one of the following passages: Genesis 2:20-25; Ephesians 5:31; 1 Thessalonians 4:3-8; Hebrews 13:4. Instruct each group to discuss and write down what they learned from the passage about God's view of sex. Then have a volunteer from each group read the passage aloud and share his or her group's insights with the class. Summarize by saying, **We've learned from the Bible that God created sex to be a wonderful experience shared by husband and wife. And the Bible clearly says that God means sex to be saved for marriage only. This is because He loves us and doesn't want us to experience all the painful things that can happen when people have sex outside of marriage.**

Step 2: Consequence Stories. Distribute copies of worksheet 14 to two groups; worksheet 15 to other two groups. Students read the stories and list what consequences resulted from the couple having premarital sex. When groups are finished, ask volunteers to share answers. Supplement their answers by sharing points from Teacher's Study. Include the physical, spiritual and emotional reasons to avoid sex before marriage.

Step 3: The Way to Go. Distribute copies of Student Worksheet 16. Instruct students to read John and Kirsten's story silently. Then, as a class, discuss the positive consequences of saving sex for marriage. List these consequences on the chalkboard. Say, **It is natural for teenagers to have sexual desires. John and Kirsten had the desire to have sex. What helped them to wait until they were married?** (Christian friends, knowing what the Bible says, discussing it together, making a conscious decision to wait.) Be sure to add that Rachel, Alex, Sam and Tonya suffered consequences for their actions—but their lives don't have to be ruined. If they turn their lives over to God and ask for forgiveness, He will forgive their past sins and help them learn from their mistakes.

CONCLUSION

CONCLUSION *(12-15 minutes)*

Materials needed: Bibles, paper and pencils.

Divide class into four small groups. Distribute Bibles, paper and pencils. Assign each group one of the following passages: Genesis 1:17; 1 Corinthians 6:18; 1 Corinthians 6:19; 1 Thessalonians 4:3,4. Instruct groups to:

- Look up the Scripture passage and read it together;
- Write down the main message about their bodies;
- Plan a way to present the message to the rest of the group using a poem, rap, song, speech or short skit.

Each group presents their message to the class. After presentations, have class repeat Psalm 139:14 together from memory. Say, **Today you have learned that your body has been created by God in an amazing way. Your body is a temple of the Holy Spirit. God wants you, as a Christian, to make a decision to honor Him by the way you use your body. This is not something anyone can force you to do. It is up to you to prayerfully consider God's will for your own life.** Lead students in a few moments of silent prayer during which time each student has the opportunity to make a commitment to honor God in the use of his or her body.

ALTERNATE CONCLUSION *(10-15 minutes)*

Materials needed: Paper and pencils. Optional: CD player and a CD with a contemporary Christian song about marriage, love and commitment.

Commitment Prayers. Distribute paper and pencils. Instruct each student to find a spot in the room or outside where he or she can be alone. Students should spend a few minutes reflecting on what was learned during the Exploration and then write a prayer of commitment to God, stating his or her decision to avoid premarital sex and asking for God's help to honor this commitment. If students are not sure if they are ready to make this commitment, they may write a prayer asking God to help them better understand His view of sexuality. It is also possible that some students may need to write a prayer asking God for forgiveness for sexual sin. They may wish to recommit themselves to His standards at this time. After about five minutes, call students back together. Lead students in prayer, allowing time for them to silently make their commitments to God. Optional: End the session by playing a contemporary Christian song about marriage and commitment.

NOTE: Be sensitive to the possibility that some class members may have already lost their virginity through sexual abuse. Be available after class to offer help to those who seem troubled by this frank session. It is a good idea to have the phone number of a trusted Christian counselor handy.

EXTRA FEATURES

Consider involving your guests in extra activities to build relationships and facilitate fun!

Games—see page 15.
Snacks—see page 14.
Crafts—see pages 15.

preparing for
adolescence
group guide

Unit 2/Sessions 6-10

I THINK I'M IN LOVE!

KEY VERSE

Love is patient, love is kind. It does not envy, it does not boast, it is not proud. It is not rude, it is not self-seeking, it is not easily angered, it keeps no record of wrongs. 1 Corinthians 13:4,5

BIBLICAL BASIS

1 Corinthians 13:4-8a; Philippians 2:l-4; 1 John 4:7,8

PREPARING FOR ADOLESCENCE TEXT

First half of chapter 4

FOCUS OF THE SESSION

Infatuation with a member of the opposite sex is normal during adolescence but is different from real love.

AIMS OF THIS SESSION

During this session each learner will:

- EXAMINE messages from the Bible about real love;
- EVALUATE the difference between infatuation and real love;
- ASK for God's help in learning more about the real love on which a lasting relationship is based.

TEACHER'S STUDY

First Love!

Remember your "first love"? Take a minute and think back. Go ahead, be surprised at how young you were and how easy it is to remember silly little scenes and anecdotes of that incredible new era in your life. Remember the pop songs you listened to that somehow expressed exactly what you were feeling? The whole "relationship" lasted probably no more than a few weeks or months; it may have been a wild crush on an older teenager or an adult. And now it seems childish, right? But why do you remember those little incidents so well? And if you take the time to mull over the memories, why do those ancient feelings still tickle your heart?

Because even first loves, even hopelessly silly crushes, are serious business to a pre-adolescent at the time. We can pass off dreams of romance, scrawled notes of eternal devotion and fantasies of Cinderella-style weddings as childish. But to adolescents, these raptures seem just the opposite: To them romance isn't childish; it's a new part of becoming an adult!

So don't minimize your students' interest in romantic love, regardless of their silly responses to the topic! Even the toughest of them has inklings of what it must feel like to be madly admired by his Sleeping Beauty or her Prince Charming. Avoid talking down to them with platitudes about love and marriage that communicate the idea: "You're too childish to understand the real stuff of love, but here are the facts anyway." True, they don't and won't understand much about this most enigmatic area of human existence, but even their naive experiences deserve our very real concern. Since they're growing into a teenage culture that has very clearly stated ideas about love, and since those ideas are nearly the exact opposite of God's ideas, your students deserve serious, first-step information on love. The few minutes you spend this session nailing down the truth about this wonderful/terrible part of growing up just could change the course of their lives. So get serious. Even about puppy love!

Love at First Sight

Dr. Dobson briefly suggests that pre-adolescents first need to consider one myth about love. He contends there is simply no such thing as love at first sight. Although the infinitely loving Christ was able to simply look at a person and love him (see Mark 10:17-21), He "knew all men" (see John 2:24,25). And that's Dobson's point: You can't love someone you don't know. You can feel compassion for a stranger, affinity with a person you don't know. But, claims Dobson, love requires knowledge.

What *does* happen when a person feels slapped with love at first sight? Consider your own adolescent and adult experiences of being smitten with an amazing surge of attraction. Invariably one of the strongest factors in the attraction is a feeling of somehow intuitively knowing that person. New-Age advocates of reincarnation suggest this sense of already knowing a "soul mate" is one proof of each of us having lived former lives. But the truth of the sensation is a little less esoteric. When a boy or girl begins to notice different attributes of people he or she admires, a mental image is gradually constructed. "She will have blonde hair," he dreams. "Her name will be something like Chelsea or Jennifer. She'll like playing tennis. . . ." The sometimes purposeful and usually unconscious building of that mental image is not a bad pastime during the adolescent years. It can be helpful to determine what you value in a person of the opposite sex.

But it's a dangerous pastime for the young person or adult who believes in love at first sight. Why? You meet a certain someone and he or she seems familiar.

You almost feel you've known the person before. And you feel an overwhelming sense of attraction, often accompanied by an illogical trust in the person. What's occurring is nothing more than recognizing a real, live person who's similar to the cherished image in your head.

What happens when you begin to discover, detail by detail, that the person is not really the same person you thought—the same person as the image in your mind? The blues. The downside of love at first sight. At that disillusioning point, you are either wise enough to sadly tear up the image in your head of the Perfect One or you are immature enough to cruelly tear up the real person and keep the mental image. This heartrending cycle of attraction-hope-reality-heartbreak is the very pattern of "love" superimposed on most of our society's teenagers.

So warn your students that even now when they feel wild, wonderful feelings of attraction for someone, it has little to do with real love since loving a person demands knowing that person. As we'll see, those wild, wonderful feelings of attraction are important; but their value is clear only when they're recognized for what they are: infatuation.

I'll Know Real Love When It Hits!

"How will I know when it's love?" the old pop song croons. The songwriter doesn't have much of an answer; and, frankly, neither do even the most astute counselors! *Preparing for Adolescence* does offer two very important clues, however, that should be passed on to young people.

First, real love is other-centered. Infatuation is more self-centered. Infatuated Irma says, "I never felt this way before! He makes *me* feel so good! *I* can hardly eat or sleep. *I* can't believe how wonderful it feels!"

Second, infatuation never lasts very long. In fact, Dobson says, the first exciting feelings between two new "lovers" never last. We all know as adults that even in genuine love relationships, times of closeness alternate with times of indifference. In fact, it is impossible for a relationship to maintain the ecstasy of infatuation.

Dobson suggests there is really only one way to prepare teenagers to know when it's real love: Give the relationship time. "How long will this process take?" Dobson asks. "It differs from person to person, but in general the younger you are the longer you should wait." In Dobson's opinion, "Teenagers should not marry until they reach their twenties, and only then if they have been sweethearts for at least two years."

The Real Thing

So if infatuation and real love are tough to distinguish at first, shall we just advise our students to throw up their hands and, like the rest of our culture, wait and see what happens in this most critical area of their development? One radio talk show host recently advised a young caller, "Maybe love will hit; maybe infatuation. You can never tell." God's Word can help us provide better advice!

Study thoughtfully the Bible's definition of real love. Then be prepared to clearly share with your fledglings the clarity, practicality and hope of the real thing.

Read Romans 13:8-10. Notice that as we fulfill God's commands toward others, our actions (such as not stealing) and attitudes (such as not coveting) tell us how to "love our neighbors as ourselves." Paul reinforces this idea in his letter to the Galatians (5:14).

Now think carefully through the crystal-clear passages of 1 John 5:2,3 and 2 John 6. When we follow—in both attitude and action—God's commands concerning Himself, others and ourselves, what will we be doing?

You're well aware of this biblical definition of love, but your students will probably see this as a completely new thought: Love is not a feeling. It's not a "something" that hits and disappears; it's a pattern of deciding to act and think in a godly way. The applications of that real love differ according to the relationship (loving enemies, loving family, loving spouse, loving fellow believers, loving God and loving self are all different), but the basic love is the same.

Love Is Not a Feeling

It's unlikely you'll be able to communicate much more than that basic fact to your students this session, but be alert for opportunities to share some of the following implications of God's prescription for real love:

- Anyone can become the world's greatest lover since it doesn't take knockout looks, brains or unusual abilities. Being a great lover requires the presence of God's Spirit (see Romans 5:5) and the decision to obey God.
- Unlike the world's insistence that the path to dazzling love relationships is to become more and more lovable, God says that path is walked by becoming more and more loving.
- Loving takes effort. If real love always came naturally and easily the way infatuation does, God wouldn't have to command us to love!

Infatuation in itself isn't bad. The temporary joy of infatuation is sometimes God's way of ensuring that two people will stick around each other long enough to get to know each other and develop a loving relationship based on more than just good feelings.

Most teenagers and adults alike have trouble believing this, but the rich, famous celebrities that are so attractive and "lovable" usually have more trouble in love than us plain nobodies. The gossip tabloids should prove that point; but somehow we still want to believe the lies that if we just were prettier or more handsome or bigger or better, we'd find real love. Teenagers need to be reminded: You don't need to be fantastically attractive to enjoy the best love relationship. You do need to be doused with God's love (see Romans 5:5, Galatians 5:22,23) and determined to fulfill His commands toward the other person. And any plain Jane or Joe can do that!

For your own refreshment, read through several versions of God's description of this real love in 1 Corinthians 13. Then without turning this page, without suddenly becoming dedicatedly concerned with the instruction of your students, consider your own love relationships. They've popped into your mind as you've thought through this material. A truly loving instructor is going to be far more effective in this session than a strictly informed one. Are you loving with God's real love? Or are you drifting into our sad culture's mind-set that says love is a feeling that just comes and goes? Meditate for just a minute on Deuteronomy 6:5-7 and John 21:15. Then get ready to tend His lambs.

SESSION 6
TEACHING PLAN

APPROACH

Choose one Approach to corral your students' interest about this topic they're already interested in!

APPROACH *(10-12 minutes)*

Materials needed: A copy for each three or four students of the "Yeah Baby, You Know It's True. I Love You" Student Worksheet 17, CD with a current song about love, a CD player, pencils, chalkboard and chalk.

Love songs. Play the song about love as students arrive or regroup after opening crowdbreakers. Ask students to name as many popular songs as they can that talk about love. Write the song titles on the chalkboard.

Say, **Each of these songs has a particular message about love.** Briefly discuss the lyrics of the song you played and the message it gives about love.

Next, instruct students to form groups of three or four. Give each group a "Yeah, Baby" worksheet and a pencil. Students work together to list song titles from the chalkboard under the appropriate message headings. After four minutes call on group members to share their answers. Be sure to specifically ask for any songs listed under "Love is more than feelings." There probably won't be any listed; and not coincidentally,

this one fact is probably the most important your students can learn early about real love. Say, **From the song lyrics, you'd never know it, but love is much more than a feeling. Now we'll find out what God's Word has to say about love.**

ALTERNATE APPROACH *(7-8 minutes)*

Materials needed: Chalkboard and chalk, pencils, slips of paper.

Teacher Preparation: Write the following questions on the chalkboard: (1) What is love at first sight? Is it real love? (2) How can you tell real love from infatuation (having a crush on somebody for a while)? (3) How do you become "in love"? Do you just have to wait until it hits you? (4) What is love?

Distribute pencils and paper. Instruct students to number off one, two, three, four, one, two, and so on. Each student answers the question which corresponds to his or her number. Have students hand their answers to you. Read the answers aloud without disclosing who wrote them. Say, **We have just heard a lot of different opinions about love. The Bible says God *is* love, so we will spend the remainder of our session discovering what He has to say about it.**

EXPLORATION

Choose an Exploration activity to guide your students toward a deeper understanding of real love.

EXPLORATION *(50-60 minutes)*

Materials needed: Bibles, copy for each student of "Infatuation or Real Love?" Student Worksheet 18, one copy each of the "Real Love Game Question Cards" and "Real Life Game Answer Cards" Student Worksheets 19 and 20, pencils, scissors, game bell, table, chalkboard and chalk, prize to be used as "love award" (heart-shaped candies, etc.).

Teacher Preparation: Arrange for one or two adults to be your panel of judges for the "Real Love Game." Have them complete an "Infatuation or Real Love?" worksheet in preparation. Cut apart the "Question Cards" worksheet.

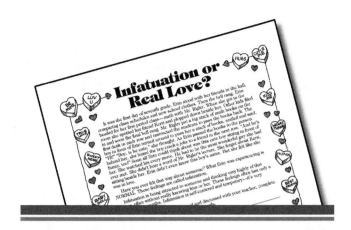

Step 1: Distribute Bibles, worksheets and pencils. Ask a volunteer to read aloud the paragraph at the top of the page. Say, **Most of you have had an experience similar to Erin's. If you haven't yet, you soon will. The feelings Erin had are called infatuation. Infatuation is being attracted to someone and thinking very highly of him or her without really knowing the person. These feelings are normal during adolescence and may last only a couple of weeks or months. The thing I want you to understand today is that infatuation is not real love.**

Have students read the next three paragraphs and fill in their own definitions for infatuation.

Then instruct students to read the Scripture passages listed and complete each sentence to discover from the Bible what real love is. When students have completed this section, have volunteers share their answers. Say, **You can see that real love is very different from infatuation. Real love involves being unselfish and putting someone else before yourself. Real love involves being patient, kind and not easily angered. It involves sticking with a person and believing in him or her even during hard times. Real love is something that requires work. It is not a feeling that comes one week and leaves the next.** Instruct students to complete the worksheet explaining in their own words the difference between infatuation and real love.

Step 2: Divide the class into two teams. Explain that teams will be competing in the "Real Love Game." One of the teams will win the valuable "love award." Have each team send a representative to the front of the room. Both representatives stand an equal distance from the

game bell, which should be placed on a table. Read the first question card from the "Question Cards" Student Worksheet 19. The representative who rings the bell first may answer the question. Adult judges use "Answer Cards" Student Worksheet 20 to evaluate answers given. Judges award points for each answer and record points on the chalkboard (ten for a perfect answer; five for a partially correct answer; zero for an incorrect answer). New representatives are chosen for each question. After all the questions have been asked, award the "love award" to the team with the highest number of points.

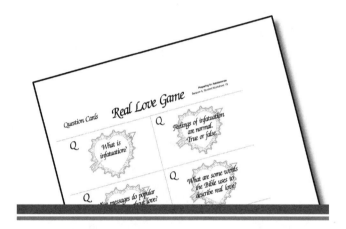

Say, **During adolescence each of you will experience infatuation. But remember, as you grow older you will learn how to love another person with the real love that involves really knowing a person and caring for him or her even when you don't feel like it.**

ALTERNATE EXPLORATION
(45-50 minutes)

Materials needed: Bibles, copy for each student of "Infatuation or Real Love?" Student Worksheet 18, several copies of "Real Love Game" Student Worksheets 19 and 20, pencils, scissors.

Teacher Preparation: Cut apart cards on "Real Love Game" worksheets.

Step 1: Same as *Step 1* of original Exploration.

Step 2: Shuffle "Real Love Game" cards and hand one to each student. Each student mingles among class members until finding the person whose card is the matching question (*Q*) or answer (*A*) to his or her card. When students are finished, ask each pair to read their matching cards. Class decides whether or not the cards match.

Lead into the Conclusion by saying, **Infatuation can be a first step in a person's growth toward learning to really love a member of the opposite sex.**

CONCLUSION

Choose one of the Conclusion activities to help your students apply their new understanding of infatuation and real love.

CONCLUSION *(10-12 minutes)*

Materials needed: Paper and pencils. Optional: Adult helpers who play guitar and improvise easily.

Divide class into small groups. The love songs we often hear have many messages about love. These messages often express a feeling, infatuation or a selfish desire and not real love. Your assignment is to choose one of these currently popular songs and change the words to create a message about real love. (If you used the original Approach activity, students may choose from the list of songs they made then.) Allow students to work in groups for five to eight minutes. (Optional: Adult guitar players may provide accompaniment.) Then have each group read or sing to the class its new song.

Experiencing infatuation is normal. It is one of the first steps in your growth toward being able to have a loving relationship with someone of the opposite sex. Just remember that you have much more to learn about the kind of love God wants you to have one day for your husband or wife. Lead students in prayer, asking God to help students grow in their understanding of real love.

ALTERNATE CONCLUSION
(10-15 minutes)

Materials needed: A video of each script follows.
Teacher Preparation: Arrange to videotape two teenagers reading the scripts below.

Divide class into small groups. You may want to have two groups of boys and two groups of girls. Show the video you prepared. Then instruct each group to write some advice for that infatuated teen. Advice should be based on what they have learned about love and infatuation. After several minutes, call the class back together and listen to each groups' advice.

Close in prayer, thanking God for teenage relationships. Ask Him to help students grow in their understanding of real love and to prepare them for the loving relationships they may have one day with a husband or wife.

Script for Melissa's story: Hi, I'm Melissa. It was like really amazing the way this whole thing happened. Me and my friend Kelly went to the mall on Saturday, just like we always do. We like went to a bunch of stores and looked at clothes and shoes and stuff. Then we were majorly hungry so we went to Mrs. Meadow's Cookie Shop. They have like these amazing chocolate chip cookies. That's when I saw him. The guy working in Mrs. Meadow's was soooo coool! He smiled at me. I think he thought I was cute, too. Kelly said he looked at me when I was trying to get my money out of my purse. I was like really nervous, and I dropped my money on the floor. I was like majorly embarrassed. Well, anyway, that was like a month ago. Now, I go to the mall every chance I get to see Jason. That's his name. He's older than me. He's in high school. My friends ask me to go places with them on Saturday, but I say no. I have to go see Jason. I'm gonna get up the nerve to talk to him this week. I'm like so in love. I hope I marry Jason some day. I'll like die if I can't marry Jason.

Script for Darren's story: Hi, I'm Darren. I like this girl named Krista and so do half the boys at our school. She is soooo pretty. She's got this long brown hair and these big brown eyes and well, I don't really know Krista but I know all about her. I follow her a lot and I watch her eat at lunch. I love how she eats. I know you're gonna say, "Darren, ask the girl out." But there's no way she'd go out with me. One time I called her. But when she answered I hung up. Man, I'm such a nerd!

EXTRA FEATURES

Add one or more of these features to your session to increase friendship and impact: **Games**—see page 15; **Snacks**—see page 14; **Crafts**—see page 15.

MARRIAGE: DRAMA IN REAL LIFE!

KEY VERSE

For this reason a man will leave his father and mother and be united to his wife, and they will become one flesh.
Genesis 2:24

BIBLICAL BASIS

Genesis 2:18-24

PREPARING FOR ADOLESCENCE TEXT

Last half of chapter 4

FOCUS OF THE SESSION

Marriage isn't for kids; but pre-adolescence is a good time to begin understanding the basics of a godly marriage.

AIMS OF THIS SESSION

During this session each learner will:

- CONSIDER elements that make a successful marriage;
- IDENTIFY his or her family life as training for adult relationships such as marriage;
- ASK God for help in understanding His plan for marriage.

TEACHER'S STUDY

Dreams of Marriage

How many of your students are thinking about marriage? None, you might say. Or a few of the especially romantic girls might be fantasizing that marriage is a fairy tale or a grownup version of playing "house."

But you might be surprised. Oh, they're not thinking about their own marriages; they don't really think they'll ever be grown-up enough to actually marry, raise a family, get old, or eventually die. But they are thinking about marriages—the marriages of their parents, the marriages of the adults they admire, the marriages they watch on TV. So what better time to instill in your students some basic ideals of what can make marriage

wonderful, why God designed marriage, when to marry and how to know whether to stay single?

Dr. Dobson discusses several myths that affect marriage in his *Preparing for Adolescence* text. Keep in mind that much of this session is more relevant to your students' family relationships now than to their possible marriage in 10 or 15 years. Also, be aware that some or many of your students may live in family settings with no traditional sense of marriage at all. Pray especially that these students will catch a new, realistic picture of the beauty of God's plan for love in marriage. Elements of this picture are:

- that marriage was designed by God (Genesis 2:18-24);

- that husbands and wives are to work on loving each other (Ephesians 5:22-24 and Titus 2:4);
- that the sexual relationship is blessed in marriage (Hebrews 13:4).

Heavenly Matchmaking

"God selects one particular person for each of us to marry and He will guide us together." Do your students believe this myth about marriage? Many young adults still seem to.

Dr. Dobson says such an idea is simply false. Those who believe that God automatically puts the right people together are in danger of making a bad mistake in judgment. They may think the first person they are infatuated with is the marriage partner sent by the Lord, and they head off into forty years of conflict.

Dobson says, "Let me stress that it is extremely important for you to choose your marriage partner very carefully. The Lord has given you good judgment, and He expects you to use it in making the decisions of life. It is possible to love Jesus and be a good Christian, yet make a hasty decision to marry the wrong person. God doesn't sit in heaven with a list of names, saying, 'Let's see. I'll take Jack and put him with Nancy.' In other words, our heavenly Father does not operate a routine matchmaking service for those who call themselves by His name!"

Biblical advice to young people seeking God's best in a marriage partner can be found in passages such as Psalm 37:4,5 and Proverbs 3:5,6. The key is obviously not to be searching for "the perfect one" but to be in close fellowship with The Perfect One who will direct each step.

Wait If You Have To

Here's another marriage myth young teenagers can dispense with now: "I believe it's better to marry the wrong person than to remain single and lonely throughout life." Dobson says it's much better to continue to wait for the right person than be involved in a bad marriage—even though your loneliness as a single person will be prolonged.

Every love-struck teenager knows it's a wonderful blessing for a man and woman to be happily married, enjoying each other's helpful companionship, perhaps raising children. But God didn't intend for everyone to fit this pattern. The apostle Paul said that it is better for some people not to get married, especially those who are called to carry heavy responsibility in Christian work (see 1 Corinthians 7:8,25-35). Tell your students frankly: It's foolish to seek marriage at any cost.

Sex Before Marriage

"I believe that it's not harmful or sinful to have sexual intercourse before marriage if the couple has a meaningful relationship."

This is another myth that demands attention. Thoroughly discussing sex before marriage may be beyond your younger students' needs right now. The input from Session 5 probably covered the topic adequately and no further in-depth exposition is necessary now. What is necessary? A healthy reminder of God's standard. It's never too early to train preteens in the basic rule: Sex is for marriage.

Dr. Dobson points out that many people in our society have decided the old rules, such as chastity before marriage, no longer apply. They think there's a new morality and there's nothing wrong with having sexual relations and exploring the body of another person provided you both seem to like each other. This is the most dangerous of all the mistaken ideas about love, Dobson says, because it has such terrible consequences.

Using a modern translation or paraphrase such as *The Living Bible,* read through the passages Dr. Dobson suggests in his *Preparing for Adolescence* text: Proverbs 7:6-27 and Colossians 3:5-14.

In your church or fellowship, be sure to reinforce God's standard of sexual purity as openly as possible as your young people grow through adolescence. They'll be pressured to conform to the sexual standards of the world system, and they're in a tough spot. That is, as Dr. Dobson pointed out in our session on physical/sexual development, kids in our society are maturing to puberty earlier than ever before. At the same time, our culture's young adults are generally marrying later than ever before. Some of your students may remain single for 20 years after the time they're physically primed for sexual relations. On top of that dilemma, these youth with earlier puberty and later marriage are immersed in a society in which sexual activity is advertised as the most natural and wonderful experience in life. And the pressure is on.

So your students are in a tough spot. It's only fair, then, to warn them of that upcoming tension and to prepare them to stand firm on God's standard. Train them early, remind them constantly: the beauty of sexual experience is reserved for marriage.

Dobson's Experience

Dr. Dobson gives an interesting glimpse into his own marriage relationship. He says he grew into a close, genuine relationship with his wife only after the first surge of emotion was over. He began to develop a deep appreciation of her; he enjoyed her sense of humor and her personality. And he saw how she loved God. He says he developed a desire to make her happy, meet her needs and provide a home for her. At one point, he finally decided he wanted to live his life in her company.

"But you should know," says Dobson, "that I don't always feel intensely romantic and loving toward Shirley. There are times when we are close and times when we are distant. We sometimes get tired and harassed by the cares of life, and that affects our emotions. However, even when the feeling of closeness disappears, the love remains! Why? Because our relationship is not dependent on a temporary feeling; it's based on the unshakable commitment of the will. In other words I have made up my mind to devote myself to Shirley's best interests, even when I feel nothing."

Dobson says to remind adolescents: Love is more than a feeling. It involves commitment of the will. And marriage, he suggests, is like a train, in that we have to work to keep it moving down the right track. The feeling of love is like a caboose that is pulled by the powerful engine of our commitment, our will and by God's desire to love through us even when we don't feel like it.

Although it will be awhile before your students experience the depths of real love or the wonderful challenges of marriage, they can begin preparing for these adventures. How? By practicing loving relationships at home. Help your students realize that real love and fulfilled marriage aren't much like dating or boyfriend-girlfriend relationships. Real love and real marriage are more like home—24-hour-a-day living with and loving imperfect people.

SESSION 7 TEACHING PLAN

APPROACH

Choose one of the following Approach activities to get your students thinking about marriage.

APPROACH *(10-12 minutes)*

Materials needed: Several copies of "The Marriage of Little Nell" Student Worksheet 21, rocking chair. Optional—costumes for skit characters.

Teacher Preparation: Choose a cast of four and a director for the melodrama. Briefly rehearse skit with characters. Be as elaborate as desired with costumes. Place rocking chair in the middle of the stage for grandma.

A Marriage Melodrama. Director calls for the cast members to take their places and for silence in the auditorium. The director appoints each cast member a spot: Grandma on the chair, rocking; Little Nell pacing, wringing her hands; Dudley Do-good stage-left; and Snidely Snodgrass stage-right.

Director loudly points out the play's purpose—to portray marriage as just a very common, everyday event. Yelling "Places! Action!" the director sits in the front row.

The cast runs through the skit very, very boringly in whiny, lackluster voices. At the end, the director angrily jumps up and berates the cast for its humdrum performance. "Marriage is gripping, emotional! We're dealing with lifelong, dramatic decisions being made here! Take two! Places! Action!"

This time every member of the cast sobs, cries, is nearly hysterical. Again at the end the director jumps up and fairly screams at the cast, saying that marriage isn't all sobs and tears and anguish; it's also happy! Wonderful! Full of laughter! "One last time!" the director says. "Places! Action!"

This time the cast laughs and giggles hysterically through the script. At the end, the frustrated director jumps up and chases them all off the stage.

Begin some applause for the cast, have them line up across the "stage" and take their bows, and introduce the lesson by suggesting that there are a lot of goofy ways of thinking about marriage—that it's humdrum and boring, that it's heart-wrenching and emotional, that it's fun and happy all the time. Suggest that in this session we'll take a look at some of the common myths about marriage.

ALTERNATE APPROACH *(5-7 minutes)*

Materials needed: A balloon.

Have students form a circle. As they're gathering, blow up the balloon. Say, **As I bat the balloon, it'll hit one of you. Whoever it hits has 10 seconds to say something about either the best or worst thing about marriage.**

Once the first victim has said something, however odd, he or she bats the balloon to another student. Don't expect well-thought-out comments; but be assured the "threat" of having to say something about marriage will get them thinking about the good and bad things they see in adult marriages around them. Also, expect the inevitable guy who will blurt something about sex; you can smilingly say, **Right. One of the wonderful things about marriage is the sexual relationship.** Then go on to other comments.

Allow just five or six comments as the balloon is batted around the circle. Then grab the balloon yourself and say, **Many people imagine marriage as a fairy tale, where after the wedding the man and woman live happily ever after. But real life and real marriages aren't like that. Sometimes life with a husband or wife is tough. If you think of marriage as a fairy tale, I can guarantee that some day your bubble will burst.** (Pop the balloon.) **You won't be thinking seriously about marriage for a long time; but now is a good time to start understanding a few basics of what marriage is all about.**

EXPLORATION

Choose one of the following Explorations to help students understand some basic facts about marriage.

EXPLORATION (45-55 minutes)

Materials needed: Bibles, a copy for each student of "The Sayin's of Ivan and Idabelle" and "What's Wrong with This Picture?" Student Worksheets 22 and 23, pencils.

Step 1: Distribute Bibles. Say, **We'll begin our look at marriage by discovering what the Bible has to say.**

Instruct students to turn to Genesis 2:18-24. Have a volunteer read the verses aloud. Say, **Marriage was planned by God to be a blessing to both the man and the woman. Unfortunately, today one out of two marriages ends in unhappiness and divorce, often because the partners got married without understanding what marriage is really all about. That's why it's a good idea to learn about it now.**

Step 2: Distribute "The Sayin's of Ivan and Idabelle" worksheets and pencils. Lead class in completing the worksheet, discussing each point as needed.

Step 3: Distribute "What's Wrong with This Picture?" Student Worksheets. Instruct students to write about one of the cartoons, using facts about marriage learned in *Step 2*. Allow volunteers to share their answers.

It will be a long time before you start thinking about getting married. But even now you can prepare for what's ahead. You can observe people you know who are happily married and notice the ways they show love to each other.

ALTERNATE EXPLORATION
(45-55 minutes)

Materials needed: A copy for each student of "The Sayin's of Ivan and Idabelle" Student Worksheet 22, pencils, six chairs, costumes for "Oldyweds Game" contestants (shawls, hats, glasses, etc.), paper, oddball prizes (such as gaudy knickknacks or an old book on worm farming). If you like, enliven your "game show" atmosphere with signs, honking horns, buzzers, etc.

Teacher Preparation: Set up six chairs at the front of the room. If desired, appoint an announcer and a scorekeeper.

Step 1: Overview. Introduce the lesson with an extremely brief biblical overview of marriage. Use the Bible passages in this session's Teacher's Study to simply point out that marriage was designed by God, that husbands and wives are to concentrate on loving each other—rather than getting their own way—and that a couple's physical, sexual relationship is designed to take place in marriage.

Step 2: Same as *Step 2* of original Exploration.

Step 3: The Oldyweds Game. Select three guys and three girls to make up three "couples" who will compete in the Oldyweds Game. Instruct couples to go into another room to put on costumes. Pass out paper and pencils to remaining students. When couples return, explain the rules of the game.

Each couple will have the opportunity to answer questions about marriage based on information from the "Ivan and Idabelle" worksheet (see questions below). The students in the audience will score each answer either zero, five or ten points. After all questions have been answered, scores will be added to determine which couple is most likely to stay married 'til death do them part. The winners will receive an "exciting" prize.

Questions:

1. Why did you marry your husband/wife?
2. What are some ways you demonstrate real love to one another?
3. What was it about your husband/wife that made him or her a good choice for a marriage partner?
4. What makes a good marriage?
5. What would you do if you stopped feeling close to your husband/wife?
6. What do you do if you and your partner have a disagreement?

Play up the gameshow format, interspersing questions with corny jokes about marriage: Life, they say, is just one fool thing after the other and marriage is just two fools after EACH other; etc.

Even though marriage is a long way off, you can begin preparing now. You can prepare by observing happily married people you know and by noticing ways that they show love to each other.

CONCLUSION

Choose one of the Conclusion activities to help students think further about what makes a good marriage.

CONCLUSION *(10-15 minutes)*

Materials needed: Optional—scratch paper and pencils.

Teacher Preparation: Invite one or two married couples to visit your class.

The Real Oldyweds. Encourage your married visitors to share with students the ins and outs, good sides and rough sides of their marriage experiences. At an appropriate point say to your students, **Whether you realize it or not, you are learning about marriage by observing your own parents and other married people you know.** Ask guests to talk briefly about how their upbringings influenced their marriages. Ask questions to guide your guests into sharing how teenage attitudes about marriage did or did not affect their actual marriages, about the differences between boyfriend-girlfriend dates and marriage. Encourage students to ask questions, perhaps suggesting the questions be jotted on scrap paper anonymously and handed in.

Have both members of a guest couple close in prayer, asking God to help each student understand His plan for marriage.

ALTERNATE CONCLUSION *(5 minutes)*

Materials needed: Scratch paper, pencils.

Marriage for Kids. Announce as seriously as possible that you have taken the liberty to enroll each of your students in a special course called "Marriage

for Kids," because you want them to be prepared for the years ahead when they will be considering marriage. Say things like, **Now I know this will upset some of you, but it'll be for your own good. There is homework—quite a bit of it, in fact. Now, I've arranged that you won't have to come here for every session. You can do most of it at home as a home study course. You'll learn what to do and what not to do in marriage. It's a pretty demanding course. Sort of like the Marines' boot camp training.**

If you did a good job of serious fast-talking, expect stunned silence. You may get several "You didn't really, did you?" questions, to which you can seriously reply, **Yes, I'm afraid you're committed to the course.**

Then, when the suspense has rattled them enough, explain that the course is a long one—it'll take about seven years. That should clue your students in. Explain that "Marriage for Kids" is taken by simply living at home through their teenage years; that students can observe the marriages of their parents and other adults to find out what does and does not work in marriage and family life.

Marriage Journals. Pass out scratch paper. Say, **We've been discussing marriage this session, and I know you've thought at least once about the marriages that are close to you—your parents', grandparents', guardians' and so on. Or you've thought about the lack of married adults in your life. Take just a minute to think over the past week and jot down one event that occurred or one idea you had that showed you what makes a marriage good and happy or difficult and unhappy. By writing it down, you'll more easily remember the "lesson" you had this past week in what makes marriage work or not work. That way you'll be better prepared if and when you get married.**

Allow just two or three minutes. Then encourage students to continue this type of personal journal until this course is completed. Students who enjoy journal writing may want to continue further on their own. Close in prayer, praying for students' understanding of God's plan for marriage.

A NOTION CALLED EMOTION

KEY VERSE

Trust in the Lord with all your heart and lean not on your own understanding; in all your ways acknowledge him, and he will make your paths straight. Proverbs 3:5,6

BIBLICAL BASIS

Psalm 22:11; 100:1,2; Isaiah 21:4; Jeremiah 20:18; Romans 7:19; Hebrews 13:6

PREPARING FOR ADOLESCENCE TEXT

First section of chapter 5

FOCUS OF THE SESSION

Although emotions are an important, God-given part of life, they must be balanced by sound judgment when making decisions.

AIMS OF THIS SESSION

During this session each learner will:

- LOCATE and DISCUSS Scriptures revealing the varied emotions of Bible characters;
- EXAMINE biblical bases for making good decisions;
- THINK and PRAY about major decisions he or she may face in the years ahead.

TEACHER'S STUDY

The Good, the Bad and the Painful

It's a good time for another nostalgic survey of your own adolescence. A simple ten minutes of solitude as you peruse your memorabilia will convince you that those were some genuinely dreadful, passionate, frightening, happy, painful and crazy days you put in as an adolescent. They were the kind of days your preteens are now moving through.

The externals of being a typical teenager have changed since your Stone-Age teenage years. But the feelings you felt—the ups and downs, the misgivings and vague impressions—are precisely what your students will be feeling as teenagers.

Dr. Dobson points out that the changes that occur in a teenager's mind are as dramatic as those that occur in his or her body. Everything is felt more strongly during adolescence. Little things that don't bother a person later in life will absolutely traumatize a teenager. "Every experience will appear king-sized."

Yo-yoing Through Adolescence

These king-sized experiences will generate king-sized emotional responses. So one of the most valuable preparations kids can make for adolescence is to anticipate and prepare for mood swings.

Yo-yoing emotions are certainly nothing new, nor are they limited to adolescence. Remember the great prophet Elijah's depression after his wonderful victory against the prophets of Baal (1 Kings 18—19)? And in the depths of depression King David wrote about feeling like "a worm" (Psalm 22:6). Notice, in contrast, David's exuberant joy described in Psalm 145. Then listen carefully to the up-and-down outlook in David's song recorded as Psalm 42:

> *My tears have been my food day and night . . . I used to go . . . with shouts of joy and thanksgiving . . . Why are you downcast, 0 my soul? . . . Put your hope in God, for I will yet praise Him. . . . My God, my soul is downcast within me.* (See Psalm 42:3-6.)

The prophet Jeremiah had his ups and downs. He had glorious mountain-top experiences—such as his commissioning by God (Jeremiah 1:5)—and a surprising number of "valleys"—such as wishing he were dead (15:10).

The apostle Paul felt tensions from wanting to do good but doing the opposite. *I do not understand what I do. For what I want to do I do not do, but what I hate I do* (Romans 7:15).

Averaging It All Out

What can a teenager do about the ups and downs, ins and outs of emotions? Dr. Dobson instructs teenagers, "It will help you to know that feelings tend to go from high to low and from low to high. . . . What does that mean? It means when you're depressed and unhappy and blue, when nothing seems to be going right and life doesn't seem to be worth living, just hang tough for a few days. You won't remain depressed very long. Your circumstances will change."

To average out the ups and downs, teenagers can learn to tell themselves the truth about a situation. It may feel like the end of the world; but the truth is that the world isn't ending because of this circumstance. King David sometimes felt utterly hopeless, but he could still tell his soul the truth: *Hope in God, for I will*

yet praise Him (Psalm 42:5). Paul could be kicked around by feelings of desiring good but practicing evil and still tell himself the truth: *Who will rescue me from this body of death? Thanks be to God—through Jesus Christ our Lord!* (Romans 7:24,25; see also Romans 8:1-4).

Paul's account of feeling afflicted but not being crushed, feeling perplexed but not giving in to despair (see 2 Corinthians 4:8-11) suggests a maturity beyond the grasp of most teenagers, but your students can still learn the basics of Paul's secret. He could feel totally perplexed yet he recognized the feeling as just that—a feeling. It wouldn't be the way he would always feel, nor did he have to act on that temporary feeling. Paul knew the truth (see 2 Corinthians 4:17,18), and the truth helped him keep his feelings in perspective.

Knowing God's Word can help even skateboard show-offs and makeup-plastered 14-year-olds keep their yo-yoing feelings in balance.

Unreliable Impressions

Dr. Dobson says that emotional swings aren't the only illusory symptoms of adolescence. Being hit with strong impressions is also confusing to teenagers, particularly when they face decisions.

Making decisions based on feelings or impressions alone can be dangerous. Impressions might lead teenagers to suddenly get married, run away from home, quit school or join the military before thinking through the commitment involved.

Dobson tells kids, "When these strong thoughts or feelings come, just remember that God rarely makes demands that require instant change. Give yourself time, maybe a few days or weeks to look at all sides of the issue. And the more important the decision, the more carefully you should review the facts."

Guidelines to God's Will

God's will as a general framework for our lives is outlined by what He says in His Word. When it gets down to specific decision-making, however, adults and teenagers alike sometimes are hard-pressed to know exactly what God wants.

Dobson mentions five factors that can generally help teenagers know the will of God and avoid rash decisions based on yo-yoing emotions and vague impressions:

- First, *read the Bible for direction.* God will talk to you through the Scriptures, and He will never ask you to do anything that contradicts His Word.
- Second, *pray* for God's guidance and blessing.
- Third, *talk to another person* about the decision to be made; discuss it with someone in whom you have confidence and with whom you can share your ideas.
- Fourth, *watch* to see which doors open and those that slam shut. If God is leading you in a particular direction, He'll work through what we call "providential circumstances." He will create opportunities for you to do what He wants.
- Fifth, give yourself plenty of time to think. Don't make any big decision while you are in a state of confusion. This is a good principle to follow throughout life. When you're not sure what to do, avoid the final choice as long as possible. You might have much greater confidence a few days later.

Of course, an underlying principle on stepping out into God's will is always to *Trust in the Lord . . . and He will make your paths straight* (Proverbs 3:5,6).

SESSION 8 TEACHING PLAN

APPROACH

Choose one Approach activity to introduce your students to the theme of today's session.

APPROACH *(12-15 minutes)*

Materials needed: Scratch paper and pencils.

Teacher Preparation: Be sure to work through this exercise on your own before presenting it to your students.

Poetry. Distribute paper and pencils. Say, **Our session today is on handling emotions during your teenage years. They're wonderful, terrible, fun, boring, pleasant and painful years. It's normal for a teenager to have very strong emotions. Now I'm going to lead you through an exercise that will help you express a feeling you've had. No one will see what you do in this activity unless you want someone to, so you can be totally honest.**

Be sure to avoid telling your group they'll actually be expressing feelings in a poem; they'll discover that when they're done! Give step-by-step directions:

1. Direct your students to relax and close their eyes.
2. Tell them to think of a definite event when they experienced a strong feeling. Suggest events such as the death of a pet, getting a fantastic birthday present, a time when a parent had to leave, an embarrassing situation at school, etc. When they've chosen that emotional event, they're to raise their hands with eyes still closed and keep thinking about the details of that situation.
3. When all hands are raised and all have chosen an event, instruct students to write a title for the event, such as "When My Dog, King, Died" or "My Most Embarrassing Moment" or "I'll Miss You, Daddy," etc.

4. Have them list in short phrases the details of what they heard, touched, smelled and saw. For example: "Blood on my leg, smoke, tears in Mom's eyes, bright red ribbon, freezing wind," etc. A list of about ten words or phrases is a good goal.
5. After about three minutes, have them add as few words as possible to connect those details into sentences. Assure students the sentences don't have to be grammatically correct. Be available to help students who might find this step difficult.

Allow a few minutes for students to complete sentences, then congratulate the group: they've just written poems!

Students fold their poems. Then those who would like to share them with the group can hand them to you. Read these anonymously, starting with your own poem. Say, **Strong emotions are a normal part of adolescence. Sometimes you will feel very good and sometimes you may feel very bad. Today we will take a look at some principles from the Bible that can help you keep your lives "on track" in spite of unpredictable up and down emotions.**

ALTERNATE APPROACH *(3-5 minutes)*

Talk-to. Simply and sincerely share a personal story about a deep emotional experience you had as a teenager, such as your "first love," an important achievement, a family crisis or the death of a pet. Explain that strong emotions are a normal part of the teenage years and that today's session will present ways to keep life in perspective even through all the emotional ups and downs.

EXPLORATION

Use one of the Exploration suggestions to help your students discover how to regard their teenage emotions.

EXPLORATION (45-50 minutes)

Materials needed: Bibles, copy of the "Mixed-up Maze" Student Worksheet 24 for each student, a flipchart and marker or a chalkboard and chalk, paper and pencils.

Teacher Preparation: Letter six slips of paper with the following Scripture references—one reference on each slip: Psalm 22:11; Psalm 100:1,2; Jeremiah 20:18; Isaiah 21:4; Romans 7:19; Hebrews 13:6.

Step 1: Charades. Distribute Bibles. Divide the class into six small teams for charades. Give each group a slip of paper lettered with a Bible reference. Each group reads the passage together and then discusses what emotion is being expressed. The group then plans a way to pantomime the emotion in a typical teenage situation.

Each group takes a turn pantomiming their emotion as other groups guess. Don't insist that students guess the exact words. The point of the exercise is simply to discover how many different emotions are expressed in Scripture. After each pantomime, have a volunteer from the performing group read aloud the passage they studied.

List the emotions on a chalkboard or flipchart as they're guessed:

- Psalm 22:11—helplessness
- Psalm 100:1,2—joy, gladness
- Isaiah 21:4—fear
- Jeremiah 20:18—sorrow
- Romans 7:19—frustration
- Hebrews 13:6—confidence

After the charades, have the class reconvene and, starting with the person with the longest fingernail, go around the circle having each student share a time he or she observed someone experiencing the emotion pantomimed by his or her group. Students may share a personal story if they wish.

Allow two to three minutes for sharing. Don't expect much expression of deep soul-searching; preteens are loathe to express deep feelings "publicly." The simple task of trying to share such experiences is enough to help each student realize that he or she, just like these biblical characters, can expect up and down emotions.

Share briefly with the group your thoughts and insights from this session's Teacher's Study. Communicate that we can expect ups and downs and that sometimes our feelings cloud our view of situations.

Step 2: The Maze. Share a personal incident of your having made a misguided decision based on feelings. Emphasize that with all the big decisions needing to be made during the teenage years, it's important that we rely on God's directions, not emotions or impressions.

Direct students to work individually on "Mixed-up Maze" worksheet to discover what can help us make good decisions and determine God's direction in our lives. [Answers to worksheet: (1) Bible (2) Prayer (3) Advice (4) Open doors (5) Time.]

Allow about 8-10 minutes for working the maze. Then ask students questions such as, **How can knowing the Bible help you make good decisions? Who is someone you might ask for advice when making an important decision?**

Step 3: Memorization. Explain very briefly the meaning of the phrases in Proverbs 3:5,6 as you write them in large letters on the flipchart or chalkboard. Help the group memorize the verse by reading it several times, emphasizing a different word each time. Then quickly divide group into pairs. Have partners recite the verse to each other.

ALTERNATE EXPLORATION
(50-60 minutes)

Materials needed: Bibles, a video camera, video player and television, pencils and scratch paper, chalkboard and chalk.

Teacher Preparation: Arrange to have another adult set up and run the video equipment. Letter on a chalkboard the six Scripture references listed in the original Exploration's "Charades" activity.

Step 1: Emotions: The Bible Study. Divide your class into three groups. Distribute Bibles, paper and pencils. Instruct each group to look up all six passages listed on the board. Each group lists the emotions mentioned in each passage.

Step 2: Emotions: The Movie. Students refer to their Bible study notes as they devise a one-minute skit depicting one or two of the emotions they studied. Suggest they use their imaginations to set the scene—whether in a biblical or a contemporary setting. After about five to eight minutes for preparations, begin "filming" the first group.

After the first skit, step in front of the camera. Using insights from this session's Teacher's Study, say a few words about how feelings can sometimes distort our view of situations. After performance two, talk briefly about the danger of making decisions based only on feelings. After the third performance talk briefly about how knowing God's Word can help us keep our emotions in perspective and help us make good decisions.

Immediately play back the entire video, which should be about a 5-minute showing. The students will be vitally interested in their own performances and will watch through your brief talks a second time with no complaints—which they would never do if you repeated the talks in person!

CONCLUSION

Choose a Conclusion to help students know that handling up and down emotions is vital to their future decision-making.

CONCLUSION (*8-10 minutes*)

Materials needed: Pencils, paper, flipchart and felt pen or chalkboard and chalk.

Distribute paper and pencils. Direct students to draw a long horizontal line on their sheet of paper and to mark it into year-long segments to show the next 15 years (see sketch). Do the same on the chalkboard or flipchart.

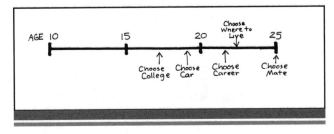

Time line. Have your kids individually think about the major decisions they'll face over the coming 15 years and mark these at various points on the time line. Suggest they consider the purchase of a car, choice of college, choice of career, possible marriage decision, decision about moving to another area, etc.

Personal Prayers. As students finish time lines, suggest they keep the chart for several years to see if their predictions of major decisions were at all accurate.

Direct students to bring their time lines to you. Take time to glance at each chart if student feels free to show it to you. (Many of your students may never have thought this far into their own futures, so they may enter very little on the time line.) Then quickly pray an individual prayer for each student. Ask God to help them face those upcoming decisions with wisdom from His Word rather than according to their feelings at the time. This personal gesture of concern for each student's future can be comforting to a young teenager who may feel overwhelmed by the choices ahead.

ALTERNATE CONCLUSION
(*5-8 minutes*)

Materials needed: A canister such as a coffee can, scratch paper and pencils.

Time Capsule. Direct students to list at least three important decisions they will probably be making during the next five years. Then have them write a personalized version of Proverbs 3:5,6 below the list: "I will trust in the Lord with all my heart . . ." Finally, have them put their names, addresses and the address of an adult relative on the paper.

Explain that the papers will go into a time capsule that you're going to keep and open in five years. At that time, you'll send the paper and a personal note to each student. (Alternative: Suggest students keep their own papers and refer to them often during the next five years.)

End your Conclusion by having a group prayer time. Encourage students to ask for God's help in making decisions now and in the future.

THE DECLARATION OF INDEPENDENCE

KEY VERSE

Children, obey your parents in the Lord, for this is right. Ephesians 6:1

BIBLICAL BASIS

Ephesians 6:1-4

PREPARING FOR ADOLESCENCE TEXT

Middle section of chapter 5

FOCUS OF THE SESSION

Adolescents can prepare for increasing freedom and responsibility by respecting, obeying and communicating with their parents.

AIMS OF THIS SESSION

During this session each learner will:

- REVIEW biblical principles for parent/child relationships;
- IDENTIFY situations that cause conflict between teenagers and parents;
- PLAN ways to honor and obey his or her parents to show he or she can responsibly handle independence.

TEACHER'S STUDY

Breaking Away

As you recall your adolescence, you probably remember times when you were embarrassed to be seen with your parents. It's a feeling your students now have and a natural part of wanting like crazy to be seen as a real person and not just somebody's son or daughter.

You probably also remember squabbles with a parent over getting to do this and having to do that. You weren't alone in those kid-parent conflicts; and your generation wasn't the last to be faced with the challenges of how kids can gain independence while parents can remain sane.

Adolescents need to break away from *dependence* on parents. That may sound a little threatening to pre-teens or teens because it means they'll have to rely more on themselves to handle boring or tough responsibilities such as earning spending money or mowing the lawn. Breaking *dependence* may sound nice to parents because it means Junior will start taking on more responsibilities, lightening the load of caring for a family.

Wording the same process another way—as "breaking away to *independence*"—might sound wonderful to kids because now they can start making more of their own decisions. Kids' *independence* sounds terrible to parents because it means loss of control.

So growing from a child to an adult is not a simple process; ask any parent. But the thrills and chills of breaking away from dependence to independence can be made less painful for both teenagers and parents through proper preparation.

Dr. Dobson tells adolescents, "You had better prepare yourself for it: you will soon be your own boss. You will decide when to go out and when to come in, with whom to spend your time, when to go to bed, . . . what you are going to do with your life. You'll decide whether you're going to worship God or ignore Him. Your parents won't be able to require anything of you because you will no longer be a child. In fact, your relationship with your parents should become more like a friendship, instead of their being your supervisors and disciplinarians.

"What I'm saying," he continues, "is that childhood begins with great dependence at birth and moves toward total independence at the far end of adolescence. During the same time, your parents are changing from servants to free people again. That's what childhood and adolescence and parenthood are all about."

Conflict of the Ages

Dr. Dobson predicts conflict during this process. How does this wonderful emancipation for all parties produce conflict?

When Joshua becomes 13-15 years of age, he sometimes gets a taste of independence and begins to demand total freedom immediately. He's positive he knows how to schedule his own time and how to judge what activities are good for him. He wants to make his own decision and run his own life. Joshua begins to resent the control of his parents, and sets out to prove that he is no longer a child. Mom and Dad know, though, that Joshua is not yet ready for complete freedom. He still needs their leadership in certain areas, and they are determined to give it to him. The result? A painful struggle that may last three or four years.

There is another dimension to this conflict. While Joshua demands independence from parental authority, he also insists on being very dependent in other areas. For example, he wants meals fixed, clothes washed, unlimited spending money and transportation to a variety of activities. In other words, he wants freedom without responsibility. Conflicts may arise when Joshua's parents attempt to shift responsibilities, along with new freedoms, to Joshua.

Talking It Out

"If conflict occurs," Dobson tells adolescents, "remember that this tension is part of growing up. It doesn't mean that you don't love your mom and dad or that they don't love you. It's a natural struggle that occurs when you begin to demand more freedom than your parents know is healthy at the time. The best thing for you to do is talk to them openly about these matters."

You know already that younger adolescents have trouble expressing themselves in words; they more often act out their inner thoughts and struggles. Helping your students to talk about conflicts they're feeling is an important first step in learning to handle conflicts.

Keep in mind some basic communication keys for budding teenagers. Advise students to:

- *Talk.* Be a person, not a robot that just shows up to be fed and clothed. If you act like a zombie, you'll be treated like one. And when you talk, talk to communicate, not to "win." Learn to talk with your parents about what you think and feel without having to "get" something every time.
- *Be honest.* When you blurt out even those little "white lies," the cover-up games you get into aren't worth the hassle. Besides, honesty about mistakes suggests you may be an airhead once in a while; but at least you're an honest airhead. Your honesty will earn you a valuable commodity—the trust of your parents.

- *Think of your parent as a person.* A parent isn't just a mom or a dad, but a person with feelings, hopes, strengths and weaknesses. Think of parents as human; expect them to make mistakes once in a while. Let them know you care about them by telling them.
- *Behave.* Good, respectful behavior is what earns the privileges of independence.

Privileges and Responsibilities

The Bible contains advice for parents and teens who are experiencing dependence-independence tensions.

Paul's letter to the Ephesians contains the familiar phrasing: *Children, obey your parents . . . Honor your father and mother . . . Fathers, do not exasperate your children; instead, bring them up in the training and instruction of the Lord.* (See Ephesians 6:1-4.)

Notice the important part teenagers can play in causing parent and teen relationships to function successfully:

1. The teenager decides to obey and honor a parent. This is his or her responsibility.
2. The parent enjoys this obedience, respect and help in the chores of family life. It's a privilege for a parent to have an obedient, respectful teenager.
3. The parent desires to avoid exasperating his or her children and willingly fulfills God's command to nurture and bring up the teenager as the Lord Himself would. This is the parent's responsibility.
4. The teenager enjoys the privilege of being fed, clothed, guided, loved and encouraged to grow to maturity. So he or she naturally feels all the more inclined to keep the cycle rolling with step number 1.

Throughout this session, reinforce to your students that they don't need to feel like helpless hostages to their parents' authority. Teenagers can take positive steps to become worthy of more freedom and responsibility by practicing good communication and trustworthy behavior.

SESSION 9 TEACHING PLAN

APPROACH

Choose one of the following Approaches to introduce the session topic.

APPROACH *(12-15 minutes)*

Materials needed: A copy for each student of the "Breaking Away!" Student Worksheet 25.

Role-plays. Distribute worksheets as students convene. (NOTE: For this activity, the cartoons on the worksheet are used only as a visual reference. Do not follow written instructions on worksheet. Students may complete worksheet during the Alternate Conclusion or, if you choose to do the original Conclusion, students may complete this worksheet at home.) Call students' attention to the cartoons. Ask, **Have you ever asked a parent one of these questions and had the situation develop into a conflict? These kinds of conflicts are common during the teenage years.** Call a group of three volunteers, including at least one guy and at least one girl, to the front and tell them to act out an ending to one of the situations presented on the worksheet. Identify one member of the trio as the mother, one as the father and one as the kid. Regardless of the outcome of the portrayal, enthusiastically applaud the performance and call another trio to role-play the other situation.

Say, **The scenes you saw portrayed may be familiar conflicts in your home. In our session today you'll learn more about why these conflicts occur and what you can do to avoid them.**

ALTERNATE APPROACH *(3-5 minutes)*

Make a grandiose pronouncement that you have decided to reveal a secret ability you've hidden from your students: You can foretell their futures. Call forward a student, melodramatically concentrate on that student's toe or ear or elbow, then announce you know exactly what will happen to that student over the next several years. Allow the student to be seated; then with proper theatrics explain that within two years that student will experience . . . a hassle with a parent!

Amid the groans, introduce the session topic.

EXPLORATION

Implement one of the following Exploration activities to help students discover biblical principles for relating to their parents.

EXPLORATION *(40-45 minutes)*

Materials needed: Bibles, a copy for each student of the "Who's in Command?" Student Worksheet 26, chalkboard and chalk or flipchart and marker, pencils.

Step 1: Bible Study. Explain that in this lesson, as in any other session, when we use the term "parent" we mean anybody who is parenting a teenager—whether mother, father, guardian, stepparent, relative, foster-parent, etc.

Ask, **Who has it easier in life—teenagers or parents?** Divide class into two groups according to students' answers. You may need to balance the size of groups by "volunteering" a few to switch from the larger to the smaller. Have groups gather on opposite sides of the room. Distribute Bibles, worksheets and pencils. Appoint a leader in each group to lead others in the simple Bible study on the worksheet. When groups have completed worksheets, class meets together and volunteers share answers.

Step 2: Say, **Many of the conflicts you'll have with your parents will center on your desire for more independence.** Write the word "independence" on the chalkboard or flipchart. **It is natural for you to want to begin making more of your own decisions. But often teenagers don't realize they need to earn their independence by showing increased responsibility.** Write the word "responsibility" on the chalkboard.

Next, draw a diagram (see sketch on this page) as you explain the responsibility-privilege cycle outlined at the end of the Teacher's Study.

Ask students to help you by giving examples for each part of the cycle. For example, when Sarah honors her parents by regularly taking out the garbage without being asked, Sarah's mom doesn't have to worry about the garbage anymore. Sarah's mom therefore is freer to fret over whether Sarah has enough undisturbed time in the afternoon to practice her tuba. Mom tells everybody in the family not to bother Sarah between 4 and 5 o'clock. Sarah, feeling grateful for the wonderful tuba time, takes on another chore without being asked; she feeds her brother Nick's pet boa. And on the cycle goes. Remind students that the chart shows God's ideal and that people will experience it in varying degrees.

Conclude by saying, **You can tell from this chart**

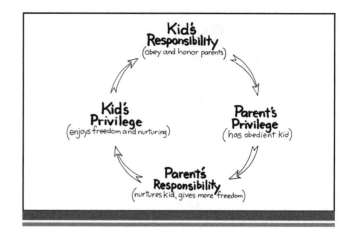

that by obeying and respecting your parents, you affect how much freedom they give you. Another key to gaining more independence is good communication. Talking honestly with your parents will help them trust you. And if you are trustworthy, you'll earn more freedom. Next we'll take a look at how you can put this into practice in your own family.

ALTERNATE EXPLORATION
(50-60 minutes)

Materials needed: Bibles, a copy for each student of "Who's in Command?" Student Worksheet 26, chalkboard and chalk or flipchart and marker, pencils and scratch paper.

Teacher Preparation: If your group meets while other age groups are meeting, arrange permission for your students to briefly interrupt the older teenagers' and adults' sessions.

Step 1: Man-on-the-Street Interviews. Distribute paper and pencils. Send students to a nearby teenage or adult class to gather answers to two basic questions: (1) What do teenagers and their parents fight about most? (2) How can they solve those disagreements?

Have your students interview as many teenagers and parents as possible within a specific time limit. When students return, have volunteers share their answers. Also ask several volunteers to state which answers they agree or disagree with.

Step 2: Bible Study. Distribute worksheets and Bibles. Instruct students to work in groups of twos or threes to complete worksheet. When students are finished, briefly review answers.

Step 3: Same as *Step 2* of original Exploration.

CONCLUSION

Choose a Conclusion to help your students plan godly responses to the inevitable conflicts of the process of breaking away from dependence on parents.

CONCLUSION *(15-18 minutes)*

Materials needed: A copy for each student of the "Breaking Away!" Student Worksheet 25.

Role-play Replay. If you used the original Approach activity, direct trios of students to re-enact the situations they portrayed. Instruct students this time to handle the situation according to principles they learned from studying Ephesians 6:1-4. Students refer to worksheet as necessary to remember situations. (If you used the Alternate Approach, students will be acting out situations for the first time.)

Don't expect sudden, wise performances on the part of most of the groups. Neither kids nor parents learn the rigors of communication and the ins and outs of responsible independence in one 45-minute study session.

So feel free to coach the trios as they perform. Suggest how a teenager might negotiate to enjoy the privilege of staying over at Housermountains, for instance, by offering to take on a responsibility. In some situations, suggest the teenager simply say, "OK" after a parent's denial of a privilege. Ask volunteers to tell ways they plan to honor and obey their parents based on what they learned today.

Close the session by praying for your students' relationships with their parents.

ALTERNATE CONCLUSION *(5-10 minutes)*

Materials needed: A copy for each student of the "Breaking Away!" Student Worksheet 25 and pencils.

Worksheet Fill-in. Distribute worksheet and pencils. Direct students to complete worksheet. Move from student to student, offering comments to reinforce the points of this session: that teenagers can practice trustworthy behavior and honest communication with parents, and can thus learn to negotiate for independence within the biblical cycle of responsibilities and privileges.

Suggest your students share their worksheet responses with parents. Close your session with prayer.

EXTRA FEATURES

Surprise your students by altering your session schedule. Switch the lesson to the opening time slot and follow it with special activities that include:

Games—see page 15.

Snacks—see page 14.

Crafts—see pages 15.

WHO AM I?

KEY VERSE

For we are God's workmanship, created in Christ Jesus to do good works, which God prepared in advance for us to do. Ephesians 2:10

BIBLICAL BASIS

Psalm 9:1; 139:14; Jeremiah 24:7; Matthew 28:19,20;
1 Corinthians 12:27; 2 Corinthians 3:18; Ephesians 1:4; 2; 10;
1 Peter 2:9

PREPARING FOR ADOLESCENCE TEXT

Last section of chapter 5 and "The Final Message"

FOCUS OF THE SESSION

God's Word provides wisdom and reassurance to adolescents who are struggling with questions about personal identity and purpose.

AIMS OF THIS SESSION

During this session each learner will:

- REVIEW biblical principles about his or her identity and purpose;
- DETERMINE his or her own unique qualities;
- PLAN a way to use his or her unique interest or skill to help another.

TEACHER'S STUDY

The Age of Confusion

One of the oddities to expect during adolescence is confusion. The confusion often comes as teenagers attempt to answer big questions such as: Who am I? What do I believe? and, What am I doing here?

What Do I Believe?

Dobson says to adolescents, "As a little child you were told what was true, what the world was like, what values to keep, what to respect and what to distrust. You accepted all these teachings without doubt or sus-

picion . . . As you progress through adolescence, however, it will be natural to examine each of the beliefs you have been taught."

You can't prevent your students from asking difficult questions or experiencing times of confusion. It is an important growth process adolescents must grow through in order to become healthy and mature adults who have a sense of self and convictions about life. But you can help prepare your students for the inevitable by expressing a few important concepts: They will at some time feel confused about what to believe, but not to worry! It's a good sign that they're ready to begin thinking for themselves about God's truths for their lives. It's an important time to develop their own relationships with God instead of riding on the religion of their parents.

Don't make the mistake of forcing the truths of the Bible on questioning teenagers. Simply present the truths and show by your life example your own belief and trust in God's Word. Students will continue to be influenced by your example long after these lessons are forgotten.

Who Am I?

Contributing to this time of confusion for teenagers is a search for identity.

And admit it—the search didn't exactly stop on the eve of your twentieth birthday. Take a break from preparing lessons for adolescents and ask yourself as an adult: What do I want in life? What are my strengths and weaknesses? Do I like myself? Do others like me? What convictions do I have about God and my relationship to Him? Do I have a sense of how and where I fit in God's big-picture plan?

Developing a sense of identity is a process that extends throughout adulthood; however, it is especially intense during the teenage years. Adolescents often don't understand the confusion they're feeling and may receive comfort as you explain the search for identity as a normal process. You can also assure your students that they won't always feel confused but will eventually find satisfactory answers.

To adolescents who to some degree lack a sense of identity Dobson advises, "I urge you to shop around for who you are in the years that follow. Go out for various sports or try to learn to play a musical instrument or ask your mother to teach you to sew. You might also go to the counseling office of your school and ask to be given some interest tests and vocational inventories that will identify your likes, dislikes and skills. By all means, don't let these years slip by without exploring the many possibilities that lie within you."

The Bible has much to say about the identity of Christians, individually and as a group.

- Each individual is a unique and wonderful creation of God (Psalm 139:13,14).

- Christians are chosen by God to be adopted into His family (Ephesians 1:4,5).
- Each Christian is an important member in the body of Christ (1 Corinthians 12:27).
- Christians are a chosen people, belonging to God (1 Peter 2:9).

What Am I Doing Here?

Purpose is another area of confusion in the lives of teenagers and many adults as well. In our culture, fourteen- and sixty-year-olds alike ask, "What am I here for?"

Again, you can't and wouldn't want to stop your students from grappling with this question. You can, however, present what the Bible has to say. As Christians, our purpose is to:

- Know God (Jeremiah 24:7).
- Praise God (Psalm 9:1,2).
- Become like Christ (2 Corinthians 3:18).
- Do good works (Ephesians 2:10).
- Make disciples (Matthew 28:18-20).

God's plan has always been for His people to share the blessing of His presence with those who have yet to be blessed. In some indirect or direct way, every believer on Earth is to be involved in God's age-old plan to redeem for Himself people from *every tribe and language and people and nation* (Revelation 5:9). The earthly purpose for every believer's life fits within that basic framework of God's purpose in the world, revealed from Genesis to Revelation.

Without wildly pleading for missionaries or finger-pointing about spreading the gospel, give your students an early start on the basic, wonderfully specific reason they're living on this planet: To fit into God's big-picture plan to make disciples of every nation—literally, every people group—on Earth.

Dr. Dobson's Final Message

The text of *Preparing for Adolescence* closes with a personal message from Dr. Dobson to your students. His thoughts certainly provide a framework for your own closing comments to these children who will soon become adults.

Dr. Dobson says, "There is a tendency during the adolescent years to feel that 'today is forever'—that present circumstances will never change—that the problems you face at this moment will continue for the rest of your life. For example, many teenagers who feel inferior and unpopular in school usually believe that they will always be unloved and rejected. They cannot imagine a situation different from what they experience in school each day. In truth, however, the teen years will pass quickly and will soon be nothing more than a dim memory."

"So," Dobson continues, "if you find yourself unhappy for one reason or another during adolescence, just hang tough—things will change. Tomorrow will be different.

"Another encouraging message [during these years] is: Normality will return. You're about to go into a hectic, topsy-turvy world which will make new demands and will confront you with many new challenges. When these stressful moments arrive—when you ask a girl for a date and she turns you down, when you don't get invited to the party being given for the popular people, when your parents seem to hassle you over everything you do . . . when you wonder if God is really there and if He genuinely cares—in those moments when you're tempted to give up, please remember my words: Normality will return."

Dr. Dobson concludes: "The final (but most important) advice I can give you is to remain friends with Jesus Christ during the years ahead. He loves you and understands all your needs and desires. He will be there to share your brightest days and your darkest nights. When you face the important issues of life, He will guide your footsteps."

SESSION 10 TEACHING PLAN

APPROACH

Choose one Approach to focus your students' interest on who they are and who they're becoming.

APPROACH *(5-8 minutes)*

Materials needed: Scratch paper and pencils.

Interviews. Distribute paper and pencils. Instruct students to mill around the room, interviewing as many others as possible with the one question: "Who are you?" Students record answers on scratch paper. Each time they themselves are asked the question, they must answer in a different way. For example. "I'm Ryan Richly. I'm a kid. I'm a baseball fiend. I'm me. I'm my father's youngest son."

After about four minutes of interviews, call the group to order and ask several volunteers to read their lists aloud. Say, **We are in a roomful of strange and wonderful individuals. During adolescence there may be times when you wonder who you are and what your purpose is on this earth. Those times of confusion are part of the normal growing process. In our session we'll find out more about who we are by looking at some truths from the Bible.**

ALTERNATE APPROACH *(6-8 minutes)*

Twenty Questions. As you begin the lesson period, ask for a volunteer to enjoy the spotlight in this simple game. The volunteer stands before the group and thinks of a famous person. The group then asks up to 20 yes-or-no questions to determine the identity of the famous person. Encourage quick questions and quick responses. Whoever guesses the famous person's identity gets to be the next spotlighted player. If no one guesses within the 20 questions, the player gets to announce his or her famous identity. Then choose another player at random.

After about five minutes, you yourself become the last player—only you don't represent a famous person; you represent yourself. Whether they guess your iden-

tity or not, use the opportunity to introduce the session topic. Say, **Maybe none of us is famous, but we're all unique creations of God with wonderful possibilities for the future. Still, during adolescence you may wonder: What is so unique about me? What can I do that will matter in this world? In today's session we'll look at what the Bible says about who you are and what your purpose is on Earth.**

EXPLORATION

Use one of the Explorations to help your students discover a glimpse of their identity and purpose.

EXPLORATION *(35-40 minutes)*

Materials needed: Bible, a copy for each student of the "Bible Bingo Board" and "Good for Something" Student Worksheets 27 and 28, pencils, markers (pennies or buttons or paper clips), chalkboard and chalk.

Teacher Preparation: On the chalkboard, letter each of the following statements: I'm part of the Body of Christ; I'm chosen; I'm wonderfully made; I belong to God; I'm here to know God; I'm here to become like the Lord; I'm here to praise God; I'm here to do good works; I'm here to make disciples. Tag in your Bible the location of each verse listed below.

Step 1: Bible Bingo. **Say, It's normal for teenagers to start wondering about some important issues like "Who am I?" and "Why am I here?" It can be a very confusing time, but the Bible has some things** to say that will help you answer those questions. Distribute "Bible Bingo" worksheets, pencils and 15-20 Bingo markers for each student. Instruct students to write on squares of Bingo Board the statements from the chalkboard. They must write each statement at least once and they must fill all the squares. (The same statement may be written in several squares and statements may be in any order.)

Read aloud each of the following passages from the Bible: 1 Corinthians 12:27; Ephesians 1:4; Psalm 139:14; 1 Peter 2:9; Jeremiah 24:7; 2 Corinthians 3:18; Psalm 9:1; Ephesians 2:10; Matthew 28:19,20. After each verse is read, students decide which statement on their Bingo Boards matches the verse. Students put markers on each matching statement. The first student with five markers in a row shouts, "Bingo!" You may allow the winner to take over the reading of remaining verses. Continue playing Bingo until second and third place winners are found or until all verses have been read.

Step 2: Student Worksheet 28. Distribute "Good for Something" worksheets. Say, **God has given each of us unique abilities. Now I want you to think for a moment about something you're really good at doing.** Instruct each student to write a limerick about one of his or her interests or talents. Then ask students to draw pictures of one way they might use their interests or skills to help someone else. When students are finished, allow volunteers to read limericks and share drawings. Encourage students to follow through on their ideas and in the next week use their interests or skills to help someone else.

Say, **Now let's celebrate together, thanking God for the uniqueness with which God has blessed each of us.**

ALTERNATE EXPLORATION
(40-50 minutes)

Materials needed: Bibles, a copy for each student of "God's Word Crossword" and "Good for Something" Student worksheets 28 and 29, pencils.

Step 1: Distribute Bibles, worksheets and pencils. Say, **The Bible has a lot to say about who we are and what we're here for. Let's take a look at some of those passages now.** Instruct students to work in pairs to look up Bible verses and complete crossword puzzles. Say, **In the years to come, you may go through some confusing times. You may wonder why you're here—what your purpose is. According to the Bible, what is your purpose?** (Allow several students to answer.) **God's Word provides wise answers to our most confusing problems and questions.**

Step 2: Same as *Step 2* of original Exploration.

CONCLUSION

Choose a Conclusion activity to help students celebrate who they are and who they're becoming.

CONCLUSION *(20-25 minutes)*

Teacher Preparation: Plan a party time of refreshments, token gifts, music and decorations. Have several parents help with the festivities.

Hurray for You! Close your course on *Preparing for Adolescence* with a celebration of who these preteens are and who they'll become. Enjoy some extra singing, refreshments and games. Then regroup to have each member of the group stand. Announce the name of the student, lead the group in applause for that person, and then make a simple pronouncement of God's blessing and direction on that growing life.

Conclude by sharing some of the thoughts Dr. Dobson gives in this session's Teacher's Study and by praying for your students' growth throughout adolescence.

ALTERNATE CONCLUSION
(10-15 minutes)

Materials needed: Note cards and envelopes, pen, CD with a quiet song and CD player.

Teacher Preparation: Write a brief personal note to each of your students expressing your appreciation for who they are and your prayers for their growth as God's children. Arrange for a minister or other church staff member to preside over this activity. A quiet song will add to the dignity of this ceremony.

The Commissioning Service. Begin this activity with a serious prayer for the great step these students are taking as they enter adolescence on the road to adulthood. Introduce your guest and have him or her address the students for no more than a few minutes on the topics covered in Dr. Dobson's closing remarks in this session's Teacher's Study.

Then join your speaker to solemnly call each student to the front. Give the students their personal notes and pray for God's blessing on their lives.

EXTRA FEATURES

Add one or more of these activities to your session to encourage fellowship and impact:

Games—see page 15.

Snacks—see page 14.

Crafts—see page 15.

STUDENT WORKSHEETS

The following pages contain the **Student Worksheets** for this course.

For complete instructions, please read page 13.

A HELPFUL NOTE:

It is NOT necessary for you to reproduce every Student Worksheet for each session!

- We have provided many pages as alternatives. Choose only the ones you intend to use in class.
- Worksheets may be made into overhead projector transparencies for the class to read. (**WARNING**: Be sure to use the kind of transparency designed for use in copiers. If the copier jams, ordinary acetate plastic melts inside a hot copier!)
- The editors of *Preparing for Adolescence* recognize that too much of a good thing—even Student Worksheets—can be too much. Seek variety in your teaching times. Spice up your classes with a guest speaker, or show a good Christian video for discussion. Even a trip to the donut shop can give you an opportunity to disciple your students!

OFF TO BUNGA-BUNGALAND

Step 1 You're heading off for the experience of your life—to travel to and live for several years in ... Bunga-bungaland! On the right, make a list of things you'd want to know about Bunga-bungaland to help you prepare for the trip. Examples: Find out what language the natives speak, what they do for fun, how to greet Bunga-bungalandians so you'll be accepted, etc.

Step 2 You're going to be driving so you'll need some transportation. Begin with the wheels—which are drawn for you—and design your own personalized vehicle to represent YOU. (If you think you're slick, design a race car. If you can handle tough things design a 4-wheel drive vehicle. If you think you're funny-looking, design a funny-looking car, etc.)

Things to find out ...

1
2
3
4
5

Step 3

On a rocky stretch of road during your travels in Bunga-bungaland, a bunch of meanies surround your car and say things that really hurt. Fill in the conversation balloons with some of the things they say about you or your car.

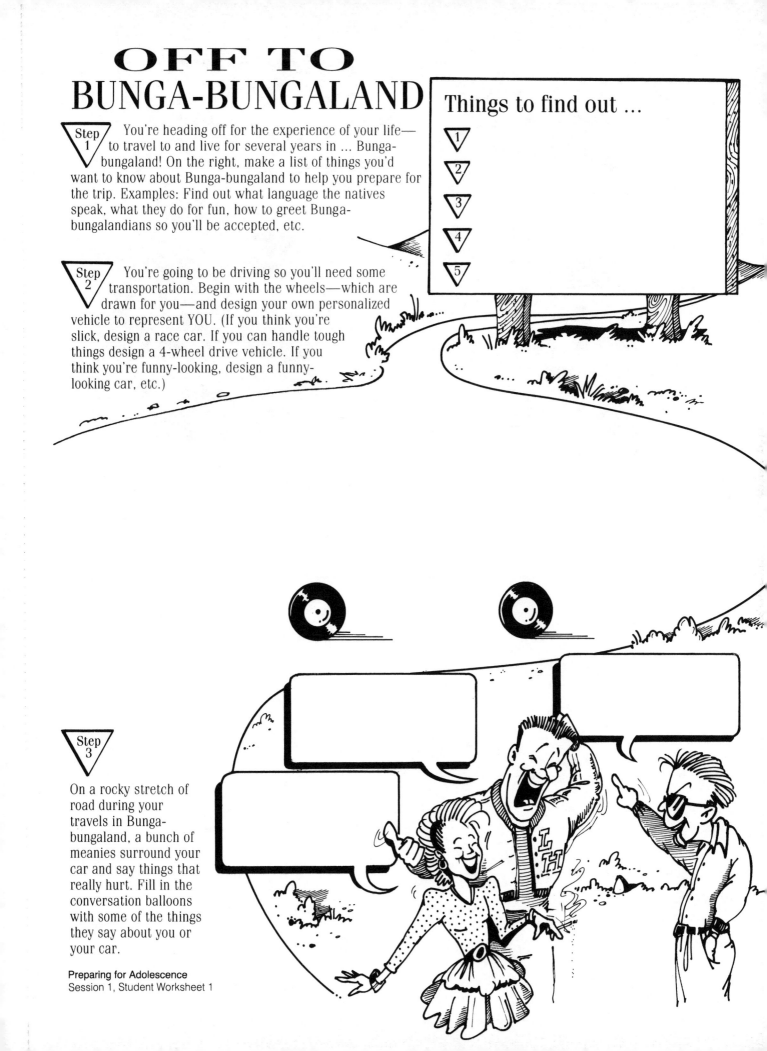

Even David and Jesus?

Read Psalm 22:1-18. On the lines below write one-word descriptions of what David was experiencing—a different word on each line.

Read Matthew 27:35-46. On the lines below write one-word descriptions of what Jesus was experiencing—a different word on each line.

_____   _____

_____   _____

_____   _____

_____   _____

_____   _____

_____   _____

_____   _____

Now draw lines to connect the similar experiences of King David and Jesus.

The
Plain, Poor Ichabod

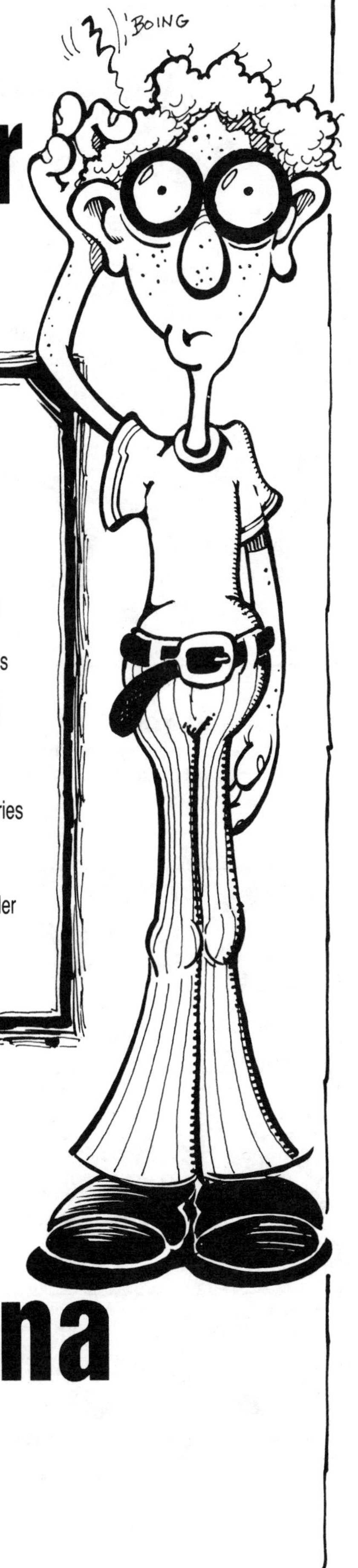

Rules

1. The first person who can figure out when the War of 1812 was fought, starts by flipping a coin.

2. Heads: Pretend you are Ichabod or Desdemona for a moment and make up a realistic-type story about why you feel inferior because you're not good-looking, rich, super-smart or extremely talented. (For example: "Hi, my name is Dopey Desdemona. I feel inferior because today I flunked three tests in three classes," or "I'm Plain, Poor Ichabod. I feel inferior because everyone is laughing at the way my picture looks in the yearbook."

3. Tails: Describe a TV or magazine ad you have seen that tries to say you'll only be happy if you've got looks, brains and bucks.

4. Keep taking turns around the circle until your session leader says it's time to quit.

EMPTY   FULL

BOING

and
Dopey Desdemona Game!

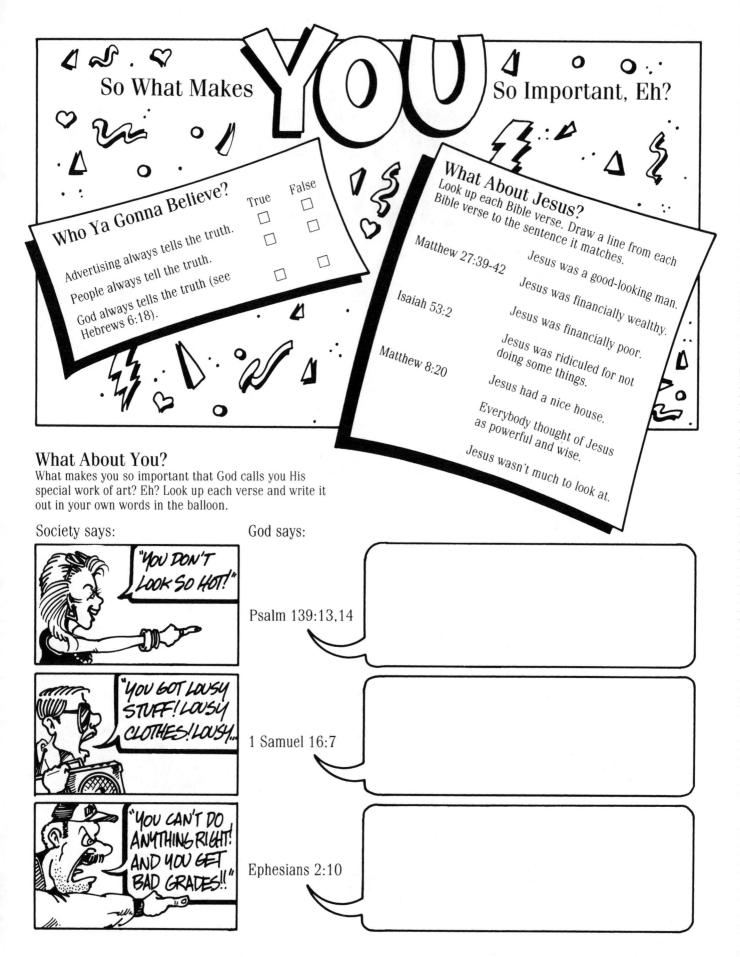

So What Makes YOU So Important, Eh?

Who Ya Gonna Believe?

	True	False
Advertising always tells the truth.	☐	☐
People always tell the truth.	☐	☐
God always tells the truth (see Hebrews 6:18).	☐	☐

What About Jesus?

Look up each Bible verse. Draw a line from each Bible verse to the sentence it matches.

Matthew 27:39-42   Jesus was a good-looking man.

                          Jesus was financially wealthy.

Isaiah 53:2   Jesus was financially poor.

                          Jesus was ridiculed for not doing some things.

Matthew 8:20   Jesus had a nice house.

                          Everybody thought of Jesus as powerful and wise.

                          Jesus wasn't much to look at.

What About You?

What makes you so important that God calls you His special work of art? Eh? Look up each verse and write it out in your own words in the balloon.

Society says: God says:

"YOU DON'T LOOK SO HOT!"   Psalm 139:13,14

"YOU GOT LOUSY STUFF! LOUSY CLOTHES! LOUSY...   1 Samuel 16:7

"YOU CAN'T DO ANYTHING RIGHT! AND YOU GET BAD GRADES!!"   Ephesians 2:10

Suspect Signs

Circle the road sign you will be most likely to believe on the road to "Adultsville."

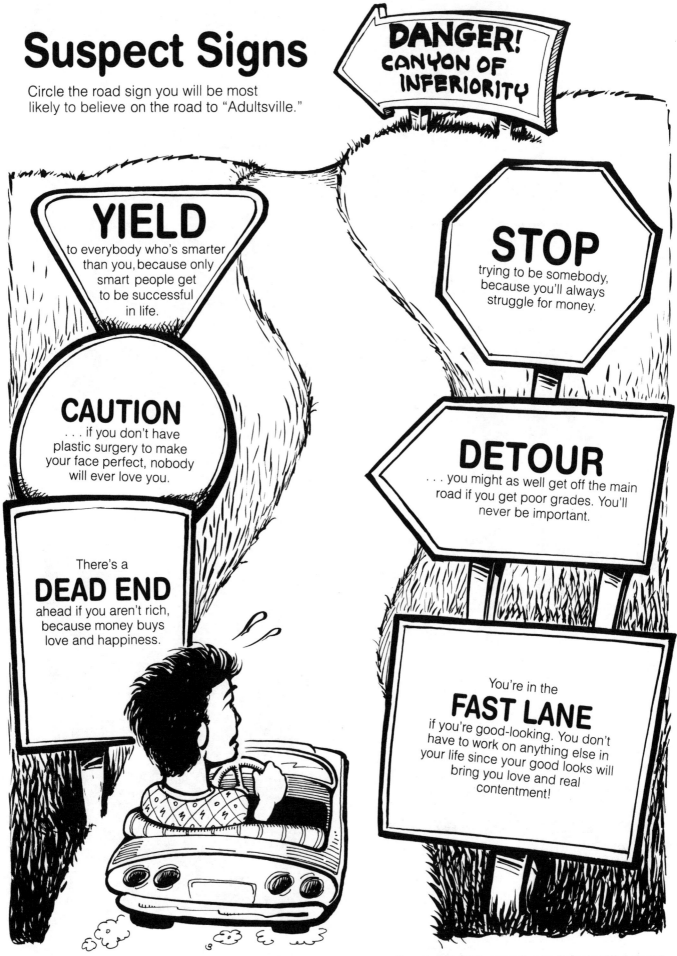

DANGER! CANYON OF INFERIORITY

YIELD to everybody who's smarter than you, because only smart people get to be successful in life.

CAUTION . . . if you don't have plastic surgery to make your face perfect, nobody will ever love you.

There's a **DEAD END** ahead if you aren't rich, because money buys love and happiness.

STOP trying to be somebody, because you'll always struggle for money.

DETOUR . . . you might as well get off the main road if you get poor grades. You'll never be important.

You're in the **FAST LANE** if you're good-looking. You don't have to work on anything else in your life since your good looks will bring you love and real contentment!

Read Exodus 4:10-14.
When Moses used inferiority as an excuse not to obey, God was _____
(understanding, angry, shocked)

us develop _____
(muscles, headaches, maturity)
Realize that hard things in our lives help
Read James 1:2-4.

N-N-NOT M-M-M-ME G-G-GOD!

HA! I GOT AN "A" AND I DIDN'T EVEN STUDY. / **I GOT A "B".** / **AND I STUDIED ALL WEEK-END!**

Realize _____ teenagers feel bad
(only nerdy, few, all)
about themselves at some time. You're not alone. Kids who feel bad about themselves may act shy, mean, silly, afraid, stuck-up or critical of others.

ERIC! YOU SHOULD KNOW THE ANSWER! / **I'M THE ONLY ONE WHO DOESN'T HAVE ONE OF THOSE JACKETS.** / **MY HAIR IS TOO CURLY.** / **BOY, I FEEL STUPID.**

I KNOW HOW YOU FEEL, PAL, BUT YOU'LL GET USED TO IT. / **I DON'T WANNA WEAR GLASSES.**

Read 2 Corinthians 12:7-10.

Realize that when you are _____
(strong, weak, perfect)

then God has an opportunity to show His power in you.

I FEEL LOUSY, GOD.

Read 1 Peter 5:6,7.

You can let God have your _____
(time, money, anxiety)

because He cares for you.

GOOD IDEAS FOR WHEN YOU FEEL BAD ABOUT YOURSELF

Preparing for Adolescence Session 3, Student Worksheet 6

Plan with your friend what you will do about the problem.

Brainstorm with your friend all the things you could possibly do about the problem.

Share your problem with someone who cares about you. Talk it out.

Read Psalm 139:1-4,13-16.

Realize that _____ knows how
(someone, no one, God)
you feel. Also, God supervised your creation while you were in

_____
(preschool, heaven, your mother's womb)

Realize that you need to _____ your problem. It won't just go away.
(face, worry about, ignore)

Also, realize that there are some things about yourself you can't change.

Dr. Schnoffogian's Inferiority Complex Counseling Services

Counselor's Notepad:

The problem (check one):
- ☐ about looks
- ☐ about possessions
- ☐ about brains or talents
- ☐ other:

Write out the specific problem that seems to make the client feel bad about him or herself:

Use your "Good Ideas for When You Feel Bad About Yourself" booklet to help you come up with a plan to help your client overcome his or her feelings of inferiority. Write your plan below:

Dear Gabby

Write a letter to the famous advice columnist, "Dear Gabby." Your letter should be about a real or made-up problem you have about feeling inferior in the area of looks, possessions or abilities.

Pretend you are "Dear Gabby." Use your "Good Ideas" booklet to help you write a response to the writer's problem.

Dear Gabby,
Here's my biggest problem...

Dear Gabby—Advice for *Your* Problem

Even Bible Bigwigs
had trouble resisting the pressure to conform.

Peter's Pressure
Read Matthew 26:69-75.

Who put pressure on Peter?

_____

What did Peter do to conform as a result of the pressure?

_____

What was Peter afraid of that caused him to give in to the pressure?

_____

When was the last time you felt like giving in to the pressure to deny Christ? Jot down the location of that event.

_____

Later, Peter resisted the pressure to conform.

Read Acts 4:18-20.

The religious leaders pressured Peter to

_____ .

What did Peter do this time?

_____

_____

Paul's Pressure
Read Acts 7:58—8:1.

How did Saul (later called Paul) show that he was going along with the crowd?

_____

Although he didn't participate in the murder, in what way was he just as guilty as the murderers?

_____

When was the last time you went along with the wrong actions of the crowd—although you didn't participate yourself? Jot down the location of that event.

_____

After Paul became a believer, he relied on God's strength to do the right thing even under tremendous pressure.

Read Acts 14:19.

What happened to Paul after preaching to a large crowd?

_____

Read Romans 1:16 and 2 Corinthians 4:16-18. What was Paul's attitude about this kind of pressure?

_____

_____

Tough Spots

Teenagers are sometimes pressured to:

In the boxes below write ways to resist each temptation to conform:

Your Plan

1. Read Romans 12:1,2. Think about what the verse means to you.
2. Circle the above pressure you will be most likely to face this week.
3. Underline what you plan to do to resist this temptation.
4. On the chart, make a check each time you feel pressured to do wrong this week.

Day 1	
2	
3	
4	
5	
6	
7	

The young teenagers above are a little confused about the changes that are occurring in their bodies as they grow and develop sexually. These questions are normal. If you have a question about sex or the changes in your body write it on the line below.

Body Talk

Dr. Schnoffogian is preparing to talk to a group of pre-teenagers about puberty and sex and all that junk. But poor "Dr. Schnoff" is a little confused (it's been awhile since he was a teenager). He would be grateful if you could help him with his notes so he won't look like a fool in front of all those kids.

△ Put a check by each topic as your leader talks about it.

△ For each topic, cross out the notes that are not true.

△ Puberty

Puberty is a disease transmitted through the act of kissing.

Puberty is a time during the teen years when a person's body begins to change and grow into an adult.

Puberty is another name for toilet-training.

△ Pituitary Gland

The pituitary gland is a pit-like region in your stomach that hurts when you are sad or angry.

The pituitary gland produces tears.

The pituitary gland is the "big boss" inside your body that controls when you will grow and how fast.

△ What to expect

Most teenagers can expect growth spurts, skin changes and to be unusually tired at times.

There is no way to know what to expect. Anything could happen.

Girls' breasts enlarge. Boys' sex organs enlarge. Boys and girls will grow hair under the arms and in the pubic region.

△ Menstruation

Menstruation is bleeding in a woman's body that means something is wrong.

Menstruation—the process by which boys become men.

Menstruation—each month a woman's body prepares to have a baby. If she does not become pregnant her body disposes of the blood used in this preparation.

△ Sexual Intercourse

Sexual intercourse is a special way God designed for a husband and wife to show love for each other.

Sexual intercourse is dirty and evil. No one should ever think about it or do it.

Sexual intercourse is the way God planned for married couples to have children.

△ Sex Before Marriage

Sex before marriage is OK if you use birth control and really love the person.

Sex before marriage can result in an unwanted child and can change the course of your whole life.

Sex before marriage is not part of God's plan for His people.

△ Sexually Transmitted Diseases (STD's)

STD's can be fatal, as with AIDS.

STD's are diseases caused by having sex with someone who is infected.

STD's are caused by hugging a member of the opposite sex.

△ If You Have Questions . . .

Keep them to yourself. Don't risk feeling embarrassed.

You are really dumb.

Don't hesitate to ask an adult you trust.

Sam and Tonya

Read Sam and Tonya's stories. On the lines below, write all the negative consequences Sam and Tonya experienced as a result of having premarital sex.

Sam's Story

"There is a big pressure out there for guys in high school to have sex. No one wants to admit it if he's a virgin. When I had my first steady girlfriend at sixteen, it seemed only natural to me that we would have sex. It was my chance to become 'experienced' but that wasn't all of it. I really cared about Tonya.

After we started having sex though, something happened that surprised me. I was losing my feelings for Tonya. I still wanted to have sex with her but the other things we did didn't seem fun anymore. I thought about breaking up with her, but I felt guilty. She was so attached to me, I knew she'd be really hurt.

It was about that time that Tonya came to me with the news—she was pregnant. I was scared, I knew I was responsible but I didn't want to face it. I wanted Tonya to get an abortion. It seemed like the easiest way to get things back to normal. I didn't even love Tonya any more. We were only sixteen—there was no way we could raise a kid together."

Tonya's Story

My parents divorced when I was thirteen and that was really hard for me. My dad moved out and Mom had a lot of problems so she didn't have much time for me. I became a Christian that year and it helped knowing God loved me.

I was kinda shy around boys, but I really wanted a boyfriend—someone to love me. When I met Sam and we started dating, I felt like my dreams were coming true. He wanted to spend time with me and I could really talk to him. I really felt loved.

Sam wanted to have sex. I was afraid to at first. I knew it was wrong but Sam said everything would be OK, and I trusted Sam more than anyone. I wanted to make him happy and I wanted him to keep loving me. But after sex I felt different than I thought I would. I didn't feel good inside. I felt disappointed in myself and I felt far away from God. Also, my relationship with Sam began to change. It's like the only time I was special to him was when we were having sex. We started fighting a lot. This really scared me—I didn't want to lose Sam.

Then I found out I was pregnant. I couldn't talk to my mom about it. And I was afraid to tell Sam. Sure enough, when I told him, we got into an argument. He wanted me to get an abortion but I felt abortion was wrong. Just when I really needed Sam, I had this sinking feeling that he didn't love me any more. Here I was, pregnant at sixteen. I thought sex would give me the love I'd wanted, but now I was more alone than ever.

_____

_____

_____

_____

Rachel and Alex

Read Rachel and Alex's stories. On the lines below write all the negative consequences Rachel and Alex experienced as a result of having premarital sex.

Rachel

"The first time I had sex was with my brother's friend. I was in the ninth grade and it was a night that my parents weren't home. I didn't like myself too well, and it seemed like having sex was the way to be popular.

After that, I dated a lot of guys, but being popular is not the same as being loved. The guys I dated didn't love me—they mostly wanted sex. Deep down inside I knew it—but I tried not to think about it. If I thought about it a lot, I knew I'd get real sad and lonely.

I never liked going to doctors, but after I started having painful urination and a terrible itchiness around my vagina I went to see our family doctor. I was shocked when he told me I had a sexually-transmitted disease called Clamydia. I had gotten it from one of the guys I had had sex with. He told me if I didn't take medicine to get it cleared up, the disease could spread to my ovaries and I might not be able to have kids.

The worst part for me was having to tell the guys I had had sex with. I had to let them know they might be infected. I felt so ashamed. People at school found out and rumors started to spread that I was 'easy' and someone even called me a 'whore.' I felt like no one would ever love me any more. I felt like I was ruined and dirty."

Alex

"Rachel was a really cute girl who had dated a lot of the guys. I had heard that Rachel was 'easy.' If a guy took her out she'd go to bed with him—no problem.

I took Rachel to a school dance. Some of the guys gave me looks that said, 'I know what you're gonna do later,' and I was feeling pretty confident. After the dance we went to a party and drank some wine, and just like I had pictured it, we had sex in the back seat of my car before the night was over.

The following Monday at school all the guys wanted to know the details. I guess I was supposed to feel good about it. I had gotten what I wanted. But honestly I felt awful. Rachel and I had done something really personal together and we hardly knew each other. I didn't feel right about it and I felt awkward when I saw Rachel at school.

When I started dating Kelly I was determined not to make the same mistake I had made with Rachel. She was really special to me and we talked about some day getting married. I couldn't believe it when Rachel called me one day to say that I might have a sexually-transmitted disease. I didn't want to hide my past from Kelly. I wanted to be honest with her but I was afraid to admit the mistake I'd made.

_____

_____

_____

John and Kirsten

Read John and Kirsten's story. On the lines below write all the positive consequences John and Kirsten experienced as a result of waiting until marriage to have sex.

John: Kirsten and I met when she was a senior in high school. I had had other girlfriends before, but Kirsten was different. She was really special to me.

Kirsten: I invited John to my church youth group and we spent a lot of time doing things with Christian friends.

John: When Kirsten and I were alone together after a date, kissing and holding each other, I thought about sex lots of times. I wanted to have sex with Kirsten, but I knew that the Bible said we should wait until we were married.

Kirsten: John and I talked about sex and decided that we would wait until we were married. It was hard to hold back sometimes but I really felt like John loved me, because he was willing to wait. Also, making this decision together helped us grow closer to the Lord.

John: Kirsten and I got married several years later. I'll never forget our honeymoon. It was really worth waiting for. It was a good feeling knowing that we had waited to share our bodies only with each other.

Kirsten: I'll never forget our wedding night. I wasn't afraid or embarrassed. I completely trusted John. I felt secure knowing that he was committed to me. Sex was a natural, wonderful way to express our love and commitment to each other.

John: A year after we were married, Kirsten came to me with some exciting news—she was pregnant! We were so happy!

Kirsten: We're really looking forward to being a family. I know John will be a good father.

_____

_____

_____

_____

_____

_____

Yeah, Baby, You Know It's True. I Love You

Have you ever realized the number of songs you hear on the radio that have messages about love? Under the headings you think best describe their messages about love, list some of the love songs you know.

3 Songs for 25¢

It was love at first sight, or Love just popped out of nowhere.

Love is the same as sex.

Love is based on good looks.

All I need to be happy in life is your love.

True love lasts forever.

Love is emotionally painful.

Love is more than feelings.

Other:

Infatuation or Real Love?

It was the first day of seventh grade. Erin stood with her friends in the hall, comparing class schedules and new school clothes. Then the bell rang. Erin headed for her first period class—math with Mr. Rigler. When she got to the room she spotted her friend Kerri and plopped down beside her. Other kids filed in and soon the final bell rang. Mr. Rigler put a big stack of math books on the first desk in each row and instructed the students to pass the books back. The boy in front of Erin turned around to pass her a stack of books, smiled and said, "Hi!" "Boy, is he cute," she thought. As Erin passed the books to the person behind her, she heard the boy crack a joke to a friend in the next row. "And he's funny, too!" Soon all Erin could think about was this cute boy sitting in front of her. She watched his every move. He had to be the most wonderful guy she had ever met. She didn't hear a word of Mr. Rigler's lecture. She forgot about Kerri, sitting beside her. Erin didn't even know this boy's name. But she felt like she was in love.

Have you ever felt that way about someone? What Erin was experiencing is NORMAL. These feelings are called infatuation.

Infatuation is being attracted to someone and thinking very highly of that person, often without really knowing him or her. These feelings often last only a few weeks or months. Infatuation is self-centered and temporary—it's very different from real love.

Based on what you have just read and discussed with your teacher, complete the two sentences below using your own words.

Infatuation is _____ .

Infatuation is _____ .

Now, read each passage listed below. Then complete the sentence beneath it to tell one of the Bible's messages about real love.

1 John 4:7,8
Real love is _____ .

Philippians 2:1-4
Real love is _____ .

1 Corinthians 13:4-8a
Real love is _____

_____

Now, in your own words explain the difference between infatuation and real love:

_____

_____

_____

_____

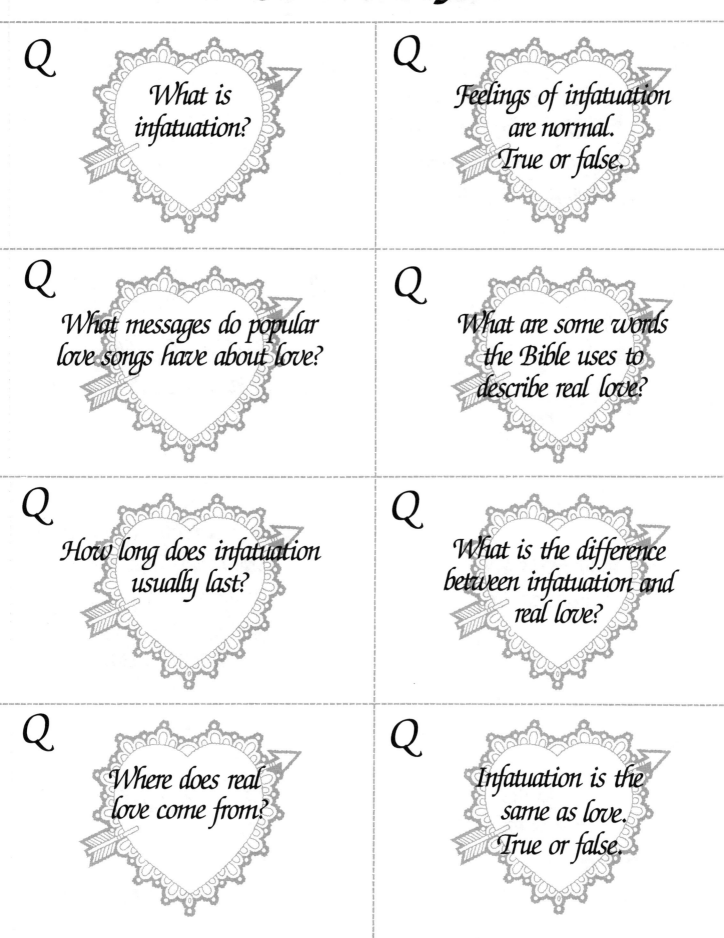

Q What is infatuation?

Q Feelings of infatuation are normal. True or false.

Q What messages do popular love songs have about love?

Q What are some words the Bible uses to describe real love?

Q How long does infatuation usually last?

Q What is the difference between infatuation and real love?

Q Where does real love come from?

Q Infatuation is the same as love. True or false.

Real Love Game

A

Being attracted to someone and thinking very highly of that person without really knowing him or her.

A

True.

A

Love "pops" out of nowhere. Love is the same as sex. True love always lasts forever.

A

Unselfish, humble, patient, kind, not easily angered.

A

A few weeks or months.

A

One is a temporary feeling; the other takes work, requires knowing a person and being unselfish and kind toward them.

A

God. He is love.

A

False.

The Marriage of Little Nell

Cast of Characters:

Grandma—old and poor guardian of Nell.

Nell—the helpless leading lady.

Snidely Snodgrass—the no-good banker.

Dudley Do-good—the handsome hero.

Setting:

Grandma's poor, rundown shack.

Grandma is rocking in her rocking chair.

Nell is pacing back and forth.

GRANDMA: Well, little Nell, we gotta pay the money for the mortgage on the cow.

NELL: But we can't pay the money for the mortgage on the cow.

GRANDMA: If we can't pay the money for the mortgage on the cow, you'll have to marry that no-good banker Snidely Snodgrass. (Snidely knocks at door.)

SNIDELY: You gotta pay the money for the mortgage on the cow. Otherwise Nell will be my bride.

GRANDMA: Oh, no.

NELL: Oh, yuk.

DUDLEY: (Leaps to the middle of the stage.) Wait. I'll pay the money for the mortgage on the cow.

NELL: My hero.

SNIDELY: (Slinking away.) Curses. Foiled again.

DUDLEY: Little Nell will be my bride. And we will live happily ever after.

The Sayin's of Ivan and Idabelle

Ivan and Idabelle Watson have been married for an amazing 63 years. "It ain't been easy, but I love the old geezer," says Idabelle of Ivan. When asked how they did it, both credit Ivan's sayin's about love which are tacked on the walls of the Watson home. "Whenever Ida'd get some crazy notion in her head, I'd tell her one of my sayin's on love and that'd set her mind right again," says Ivan.

Read each of Ivan and Idabelle's sayin's about love. Then read the paragraphs below. Write the letter of each paragraph by its matching sign on the Watson's walls.

It's better to be all alone, than to be married to a drone.

Love's not instant, no siree,

But work at love and more you'll see!

Sex is meant for man and wife, At other times it leads to strife.

A love-at-first-sight situation, is nothing but infatuation.

Love is not "Give me! Give me!" It's "Can I help? What do you need?"

Folks, don't marry on a whim, 'Cause you'll be stuck with her or him.

When couples "fuss" and "carry on," It doesn't mean that love is gone.

a. Infatuation is a strong attraction to a member of the opposite sex that often occurs before you really know the person. It feels like "love" but it is not love. Infatuation is a feeling that often lasts only several weeks or months.

b. Real love is caring about another person as much as you care about yourself. Real love involves being unselfish, patient, kind, not easily angered and thinking about the interests of the other person. Real love is not easy—it takes work.

c. God wants us to use good sense when choosing a marriage partner, rather than making a hasty decision based on a feeling or impression. You should take your time and really get to know the person before you decide to get married. Dr. Dobson says, "Choose your mate very carefully *after* your twentieth birthday."

d. Being single is lonely at times but that's no reason to marry just anyone. Marrying a person you don't really love can lead to divorce or a lifetime of living with someone you don't get along with.

e. Sexual intercourse is meant to take place within marriage. Sex outside of marriage can lead to unwanted children, diseases and emotional pain.

f. Once you marry, love is not automatic. Sometimes you'll feel close to your mate and sometimes you won't. But you can work at showing love no matter how you feel.

g. People who genuinely love each other still disagree and may sometimes get into arguments. When this happens it means they need to work together to find a solution to their problems.

What's Wrong with This Picture?

Read each of the cartoons below. Then choose one of the cartoons to write about. Using some of the facts you have learned about marriage, explain what is wrong in the picture.

_____

_____

_____

_____

_____

Mixed-up Maze

As you grow up you will be making more and more decisions. Making decisions based only on how you feel is not a good idea because:
- feelings change,
- feelings can distort the way you view a situation.

Follow the maze below and unscramble the words along the path to find five important things that will help you make good decisions. Write the words in the spaces provided.

1. ___ ___ ___ ___ ___ ___ ___   2. ___ ___ ___ ___ ___ ___ ___ ___ ___   3. ___ ___ ___ ___ ___ ___ ___

4. ___ ___ ___ ___ ___ ___ ___ ___ ___ ___ ___ ___ ___ ___   5. ___ ___ ___ ___ ___ ___

Breaking Away!

Circle the question or statement most likely to cause conflict between you and a parent. Finish the cartoon by filling in:

• how your parent usually responds,

• how you could respond if you were obeying the commands in Ephesians 6:1-3.

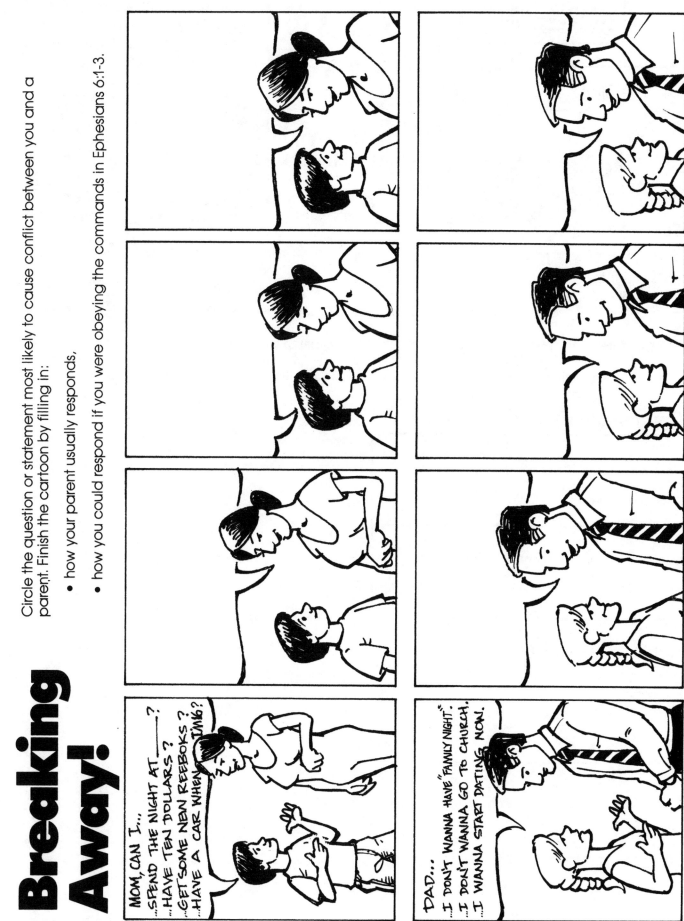

MOM, CAN I...
...SPEND THE NIGHT AT _____ ?
...HAVE TEN DOLLARS ?
...GET SOME NEW REEBOKS ?
...HAVE A CAR WHEN I'M 16?

DAD...
...I DON'T WANNA HAVE "FAMILY NIGHT".
...I DON'T WANNA GO TO CHURCH.
...I WANNA START DATING NOW.

Who's in Command ?

Your parents are used to being in command. But now you want to be "in command." Find out how things are supposed to work when God is in command—look up and read Ephesians 6:1-4. In the boxes below, write the four commands found in the passage. Beside each command, list a few ways to obey that command.

Commands to Kids

Commands to Parents

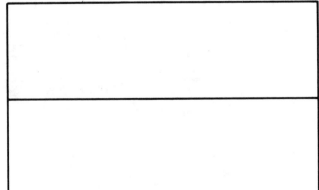

Bible Bingo Board

		FREE		

Good for Something!

The Bible says you are a unique creation of God!

Write a limerick about one of your interests or talents.
(A limerick is a special kind of poem with five lines and a certain number of syllables.)

Example:
There once was a boy known as Bill.
To him, cracking jokes was a thrill.
When Bill was a-lurking,
You'd soon be a-smirking.
'Cause making folks laugh was Bill's skill.

_____ (8 syllables)

_____ (8 syllables)

_____ (6 syllables)

_____ (6 syllables)

_____ (8 syllables)

The Bible says you are an important member of the Body of Christ! Draw a picture of one way you can use your interest or talent to help someone.

Example:

Bill helping out with Sunday School...

God's Word Crossword

Have you ever wondered who you are and what you're doing here? Look up the verses listed below and fill in the crossword puzzle to discover who God made you to be and what He wants you to do.

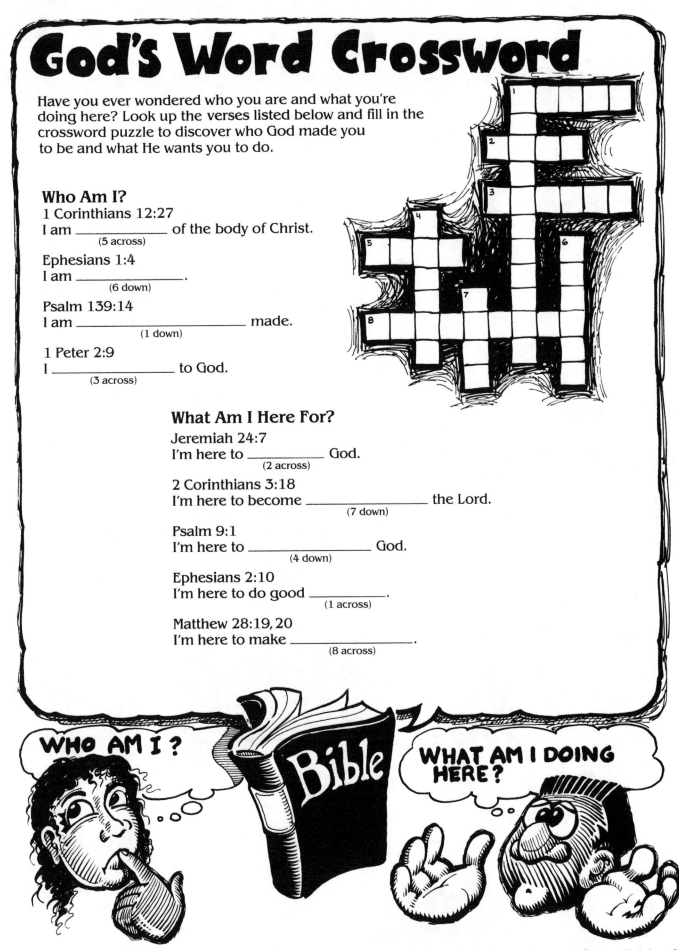

Who Am I?

1 Corinthians 12:27
I am _____ of the body of Christ.
(5 across)

Ephesians 1:4
I am _____.
(6 down)

Psalm 139:14
I am _____ made.
(1 down)

1 Peter 2:9
I _____ to God.
(3 across)

What Am I Here For?

Jeremiah 24:7
I'm here to _____ God.
(2 across)

2 Corinthians 3:18
I'm here to become _____ the Lord.
(7 down)

Psalm 9:1
I'm here to _____ God.
(4 down)

Ephesians 2:10
I'm here to do good _____.
(1 across)

Matthew 28:19, 20
I'm here to make _____.
(8 across)

WHO AM I ?

Bible

WHAT AM I DOING HERE?

DESIGN-IT-YOURSELF SECTION!

The following pages contain all sorts of fun artwork. Use them for mail outs, bulletins, and overhead projector transparencies. Cut 'em out, past 'em up, and there you have it!

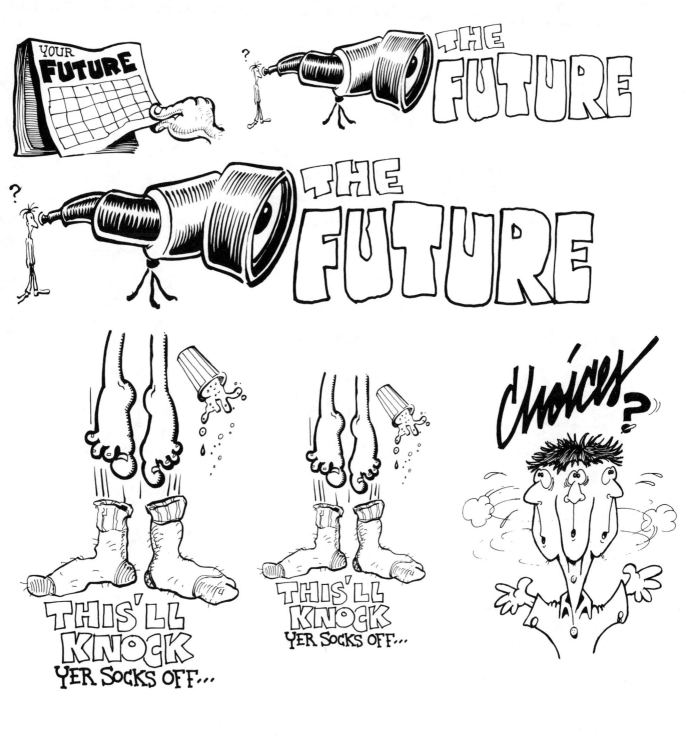

Dear Parents,

Your child will have the opportunity to participate in a 10-session course based on a book by Dr. James Dobson called *Preparing for Adolescence.* The purpose of this course is to provide biblically-based insights which can help adolescents as they grow to adulthood.

During this course students will cover the following topics:

- how to handle feelings of inferiority
- how to develop self-confidence
- how to handle group pressure to conform
- how to say no to drugs and alcohol
- physical and sexual development
- the meaning of real love
- how to handle emotions
- how to make sound decisions
- understanding normal independence
- basics of self-identity

Session five of this course deals with sexual development and its accompanying responsibilities. Because of the sensitive nature of this topic, only students with parental consent will be allowed to participate.

To give permission for your child to participate in this course, please sign and return the form below.

Sincerely,

My child, _____, has my permission to attend the *Preparing for Adolescence* course to be held

Date: _____   Time: _____
Place: _____

_____

_____   _____
              signed   date

INTRODUCING YOUNG PEOPLE TO CHRIST

How do you present Christ to a young person?

1. PRAY. Ask God to prepare the young person to receive the message, and pray about exactly how you can present that good news.

2. LAY THE FOUNDATION. Youth are evaluating you and the Lord you serve by everything you do and say. They are looking for people whose lives say knowing God makes a noticeable difference, for people who love them and listen to them the same way God loves them and listens to them.

Learn to listen with your full attention. Learn to share honestly both the joys and the struggles you encounter as a Christian. Learn to accept kids as they are. Christ died for them while they were yet sinners. You are also called to love them as they are.

3. BE AWARE OF OPPORTUNITIES. A student may hint around and hang around to talk after class. Or some might be waiting for you to suggest going for a Coke. Get alone together where you can share what Jesus Christ means to you.

4. HAVE A PLAN. Don't lecture or force the issue. Here are some tips to keep in mind:

- *Put the student at ease.* Remember he or she is probably nervous. Be relaxed, natural and casual in your conversation, not critical or judgmental.
- *Get him or her to talk,* and listen carefully to what is said. Students may make superficial or shocking statements just to get a reaction. Don't begin lecturing or problem-solving. Instead encourage him or her to keep talking.
- *Be gently direct.* Students may have trouble bringing up topics they're seriously con-

cerned about. If you sense this, a simple question like, "How are you and God getting along?" or, "What are your feelings about God lately?" can unlock a life-changing conversation.

- *Discuss God's desire to have fellowship with people.* As you relate God's plan for enabling people to have a relationship with Him, move through the points slowly enough to allow time for thinking and understanding. However, don't drag out the presentation.

    a. God's goal for us is abundant life (John 3:16; John 10:10). God wants to bless us so we can in turn bless others.
    b. All people are separated from God by sin (Romans 3:23: Romans 6:23).
    c. God's only solution is Jesus Christ who died to pay the penalty for our sin (Romans 5:8; John 14:6).
    d. Our response is to repent (turn from

our sins) and receive Christ as Savior (John 1:12; Acts 3:19).

- *Make sure the student understands* that accepting Christ is very simple, but also following Christ involves obedience to His Lordship; the abundant life is a demanding life. This is not a snap decision to be made and then forgotten. If you feel the student understands, ask if he or she would like to accept Christ now. If so, ask the student to pray with you. Explain that praying is simply talking to God. In this case it's telling God of the student's need for Christ and desire for Christ to be his or her personal Savior and Lord.

After prayer, begin confirming the decision by reading assurance passages such as Revelation 3:20. Assurance of salvation is elusive to many young teenagers since they often react emotionally rather than by faith in what God says. Suggest this new believer learn as much as possible to grow in the faith. *How to Be a Christian Without Being Religious* by Fritz Ridenour (Regal Books) is a good book to begin with.

If your young person feels unready to make a decision, suggest some Scripture to read and make an appointment to get together again. John 14—16, Romans 3—8 and the Gospel of Mark are good sections for reading.

5. REMEMBER that your responsibility is simply to present the gospel and to be able to explain the hope that is within you. It is the Holy Spirit who makes the heart ready for a relationship with God and gives growth.

WHEN IT'S ALL SAID AND DONE (FOLLOW-UP)

When it's all said and done, what is done will far outlast what is said.

The time you invest in building relationships, encouraging and affirming students, listening to them and putting up with their rowdy moods (which seem to be never ending) will pay dividends in the Kingdom of God.

You may be the world's best teacher, but face it: It's the personal touch that will win your kids' hearts. They know when someone cares for them. And that caring pays off.

Relationships don't have to end with the packing away of materials. Be sure to plan for follow-up contacts with each of your students even after they've outgrown this *Preparing for Adolescence* material.

Immediately follow up on those who become Christians. Get them into Sunday School. Visit their homes to answer questions and give encouragement. Provide transportation when needed.

Plan follow-up for those who re-dedicate their lives to the Lord: They need guidance in Bible study, in prayer and in preparing for the work the Lord has for them.

Plan follow-up for the unsaved: Invite them to church youth activities. Bring them to Sunday School and worship services. Continue to pray for them by name. Remember their birthdays with a card or phone call.

Plan follow-up for unchurched parents: Show genuine interest in their young people. Continue to invite the entire family to church services and church activities—especially to adult Bible classes.

And when that once ornery kid begins to respond to the love and caring you have shown, don't be surprised if he or she thinks about you and what you did to demonstrate God's love—and tries to do the same for someone else!

Preparation Is Key for Adolescence

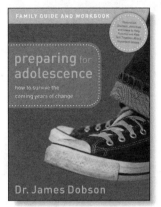

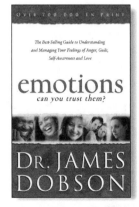
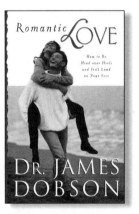
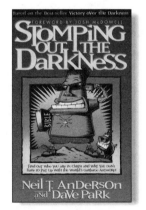